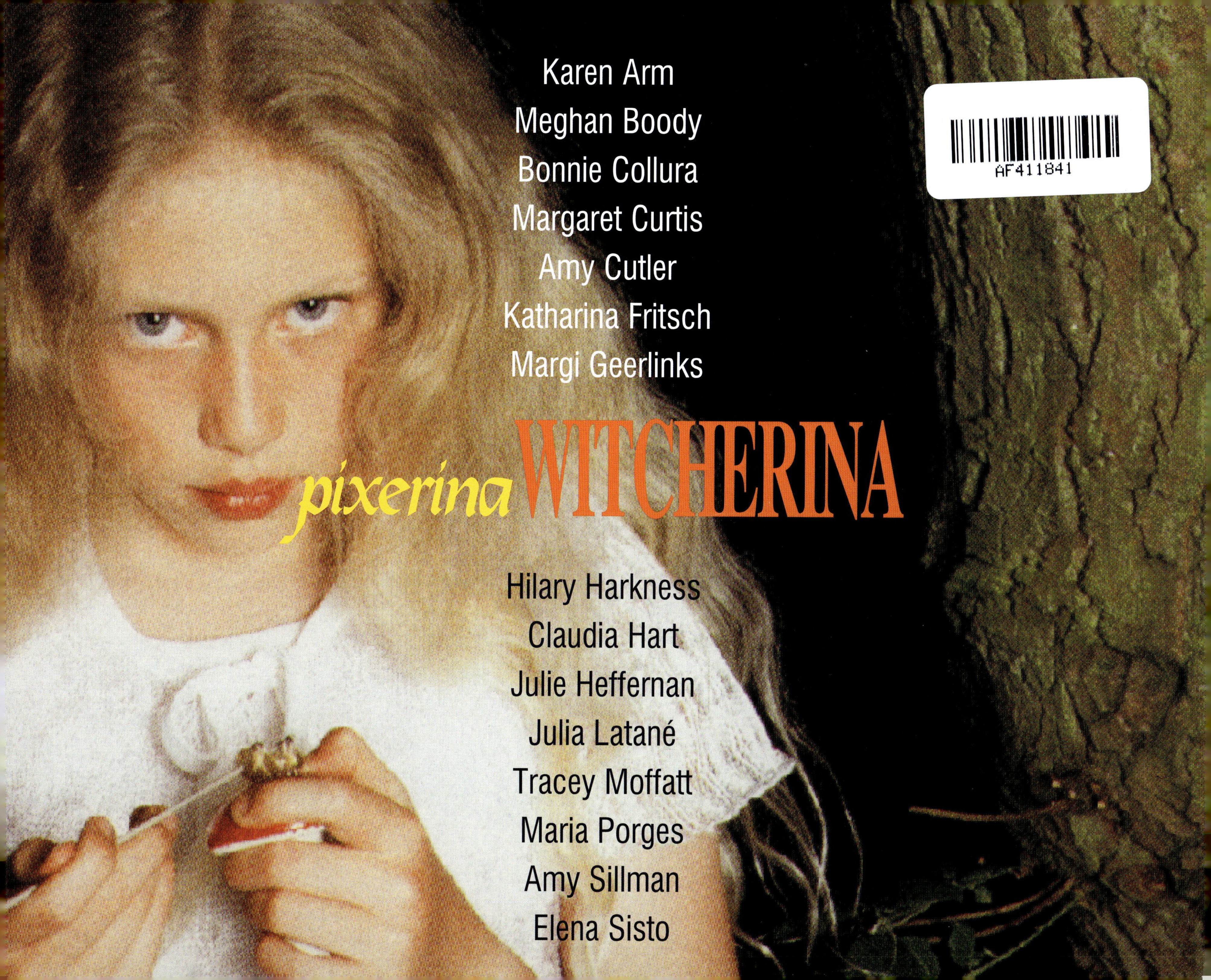

Karen Arm
Meghan Boody
Bonnie Collura
Margaret Curtis
Amy Cutler
Katharina Fritsch
Margi Geerlinks

pixerina WITCHERINA

Hilary Harkness
Claudia Hart
Julie Heffernan
Julia Latané
Tracey Moffatt
Maria Porges
Amy Sillman
Elena Sisto

AF411841

pixerina **WITCHERINA** was curated by Bill Conger.

© 2002 University Galleries of Illinois State University. All rights reserved.
© 2002 Bill Conger, WHAT BIG TEETH
© 2002 Maria Tatar, INVOCATIONS OF FAIRY TALES
© 2002 Jan Susina, STRAW INTO GOLD: THE TRANSFORMATIVE NATURE OF FAIRY TALES AND FAIRY ART
All reproductions of artwork © of the artists

Design: Bill Conger and Barry Blinderman
Editors: Barry Blinderman and Timothy Porges
Production assistance: Matt Pulford and Karl Rademacher
Publisher: University Galleries of Illinois State University
Distributor: Distributed Art Publishers, New York   tel 800.338.2665
Printing: Original Smith Printing Inc., Normal, Illinois

Cover: Meghan Boody, PSYCHE'S TAIL detail, 1998. Fujiflex print. Photo: Ted Diamond.
Courtesy Sandra Gering Gallery, New York.
Frontispiece: Margi Geerlinks, UNTITLED (GIRL) detail, 1999. Fujichrome, perspex, and
dibond, 60 x 49 1/4 inches. Courtesy Stefan Stux Gallery, New York.

This publication has been supported in part by a
grant from the Illinois Arts Council, a state agency

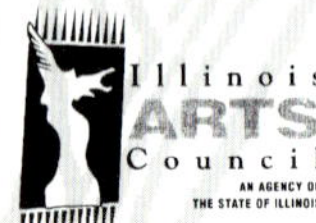

university
galleries

illinois state university
campus box 5620
normal, il 61790-5620

www.orat.ilstu.edu/cfa/galleries
gallery@oratmail.cfa.ilstu.edu
tel   309.438.5487
fax   309.438.5161

ISBN 0-945558-31-7

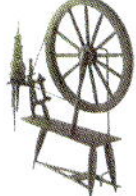

WHAT BIG TEETH
Bill Conger

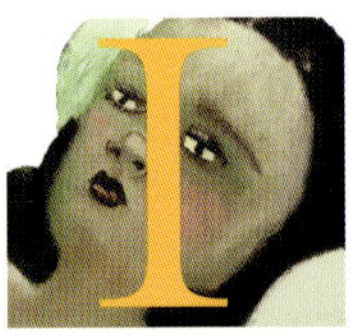 remember looking on as my grandmother turned the worn Golden Book pages. The images within impressed me indelibly. I can still see Gretel slamming the oven door on the witch's twisted feet, death-pallored Snow White encased in her glass coffin, and Princess Aurora's pricked finger oozing magenta-tinged blood—grotesque images that were entrancing, horrific, and mesmerizing.

Like the candy cottage that conceals the oven, fairy tales conceal a darker world, and as they are told to children, that darkness inevitably leaks into the telling as if by accident. Most disturbing to my childhood were the evil maternal figures—child-eating witches, grandmothers with big teeth, evil stepmothers and assorted hags and crones. Drifting in and out of reverie, I would wonder if Grandma might, when not reading to me, secretly become a murderous witch planning my demise.

Recent experiences have returned me to the fossil remnants of those daydreams. One night singing Rock-a-Bye Baby, I realized that in essence I had been threatening my sons, telling them they might fall to their deaths from a treetop. Awakening to the cruelty wrapped in that familiar, music-box melody led me back to fairy tales.

once upon a time . . .

Children's literature is part of children's culture, and folktales are part of that; not the public, social part, maybe, but the part each child keeps secret, and dreams about.

The tales might have been thought of, once, as having some usefulness in preparing children for a harsh and dangerous world, in which there is no tie of trust between the large and the small, or between men and women. But the world the folktales frame now, as a kind of darkness at the edge of things, is the world of childhood itself.

Before the Brothers Grimm documented some of today's popular European folk tales stories, the oldest tales existed in the oral tradition like living, breathing matter, slightly transfigured from telling to telling. In contemporary art many women are keeping the organic essence of fairy tales alive—using, retelling, and merging the symbolic content into contemporary myth new and improved. The artists in this exhibit draw on those fabulous fears of childhood, its darkness and mistrust, as a living cultural legacy.

the little girl and the big bad woolf

"Pixerina witcherina" was an invented language, made up out of odd and exotic sounds—definitely non-English—used by Virginia Woolf to converse secretly with her niece.[1] As a code, its primary secret was the identity of its users—that secretly they weren't just aunt and niece, but they were also pixies and witches. Pixie and Witch represent two possible halves of a split female identity: young / old, innocent / sexual, free / powerful. Witch and Pixie bracket the socially normal "feminine." Your mom is not a witch or a pixie, but your fey Aunt Virginia just might be either. The lost arcadia of prepubescence is something we recall in artwork, with

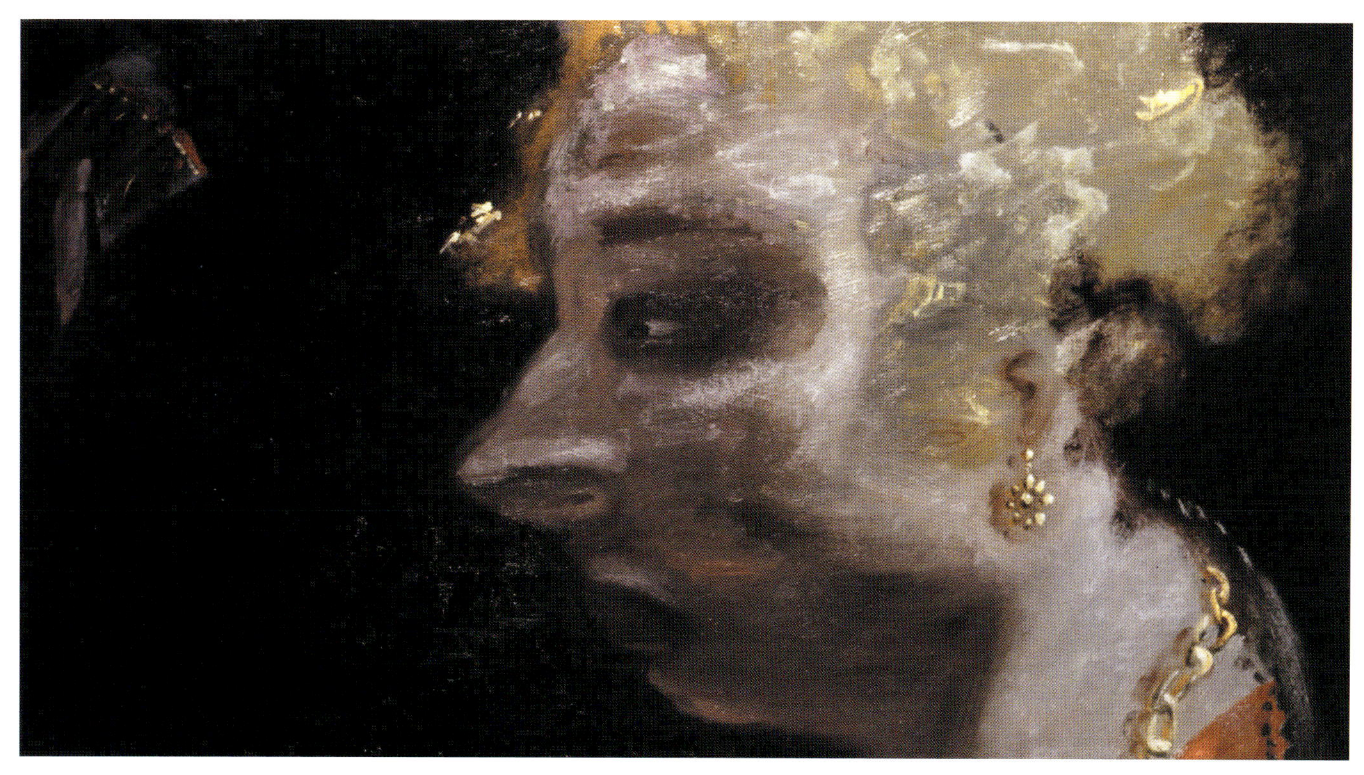

Elena Sisto, NOGUE, 1998
Oil on linen, 26 x 48 inches
Courtesy the artist

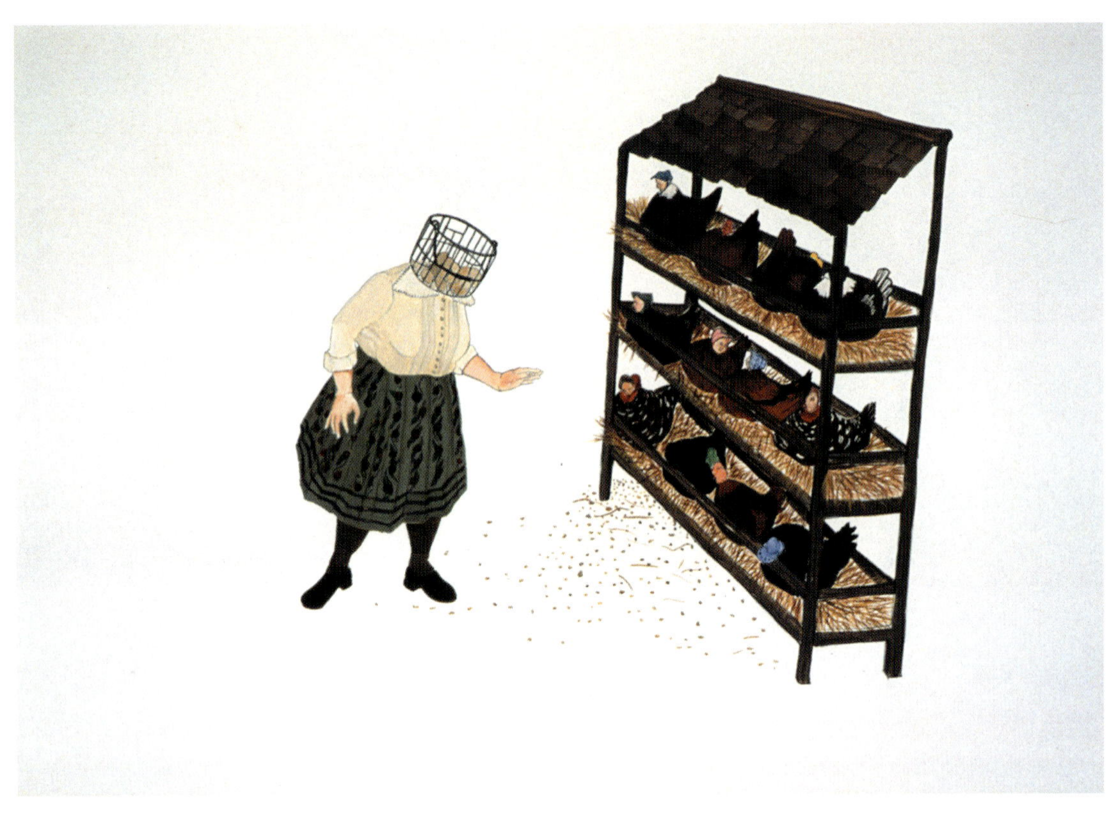

Amy Cutler, EGG COLLECTION, 1999
Gouache on paper, 16 1/2 x 22 3/4 inches
Courtesy Eyewash, Williamsburg, NY

nostalgia and regret. And sometimes, like during the Sixties and what remains of them in the culture, Pixie and Witch, like Virgin and Whore, can seem less like the imposed binaries of an overbearing patriarchy than like an intriguing group of possible future career choices for the enterprising little girl to consider.

*pixerina*WITCHERINA is then, both about the youth-culture of Future Goddesses and about the shared, subversive culture of women, old and young. Meghan Boody's *Through the Looking Glass*-inspired photographic narratives in which a young girl, Psyche, encounters her alter ego, Smut, Margi Geerlinks' photographs of old women and nymphlike girls, Julie Heffernan's goddess-like self-portrait, and Hilary Harkness' Amazonian no man's lands offer us female protagonists who draw from the full menu of choices: virgin (the huntress and the sorrowing virgin; not the same at all, but each fun in its own way), nymph (sometimes a whore,but not always) and crone.

a little change

Moral lessons in fairy tales are also lessons in magic. And these lessons in magic are what prepare us for the metamorphoses of adolescence, and then, adulthood. Marina Warner identifies these transformations as metaphors for enlightenment, in which changes of shape "constitute the fundamental principle of nature, a rationale for its mysteries."[2] And the inevitability of these transformations, as it drives the narrative of the folktale, is also instructive: a frog has to turn into a prince, just as children have to grow up and become their parents.

These recurrent shape-shiftings are a regular feature of both folktale and the work in this show. In Bonnie Collura's orgy of forms and identities, THE PURSUIT OF HAPPINESS, human and animal forms (and even the cartoon presence of Mickey Mouse) bubble out to the surface. Megan Boody's characters, Psyche and Smut, are part rat, part reptile, even part insect. And in Amy Cutler's

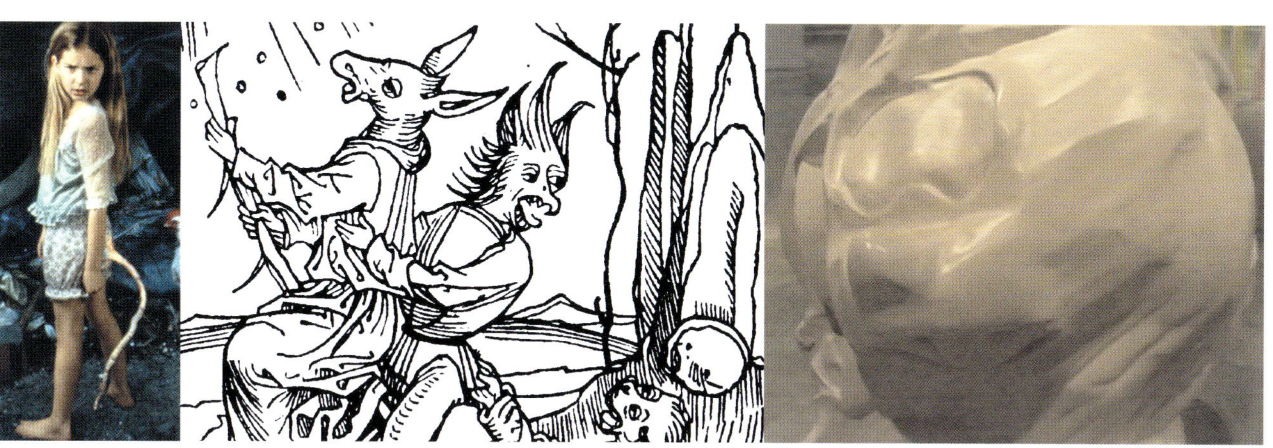

Meghan Boody, PSYCHE'S TAIL detail, 2000. Courtesy Sandra Gering Gallery, New York.

Illustration detail of three witches changing shape and flying on a broomstick. From Ulrich Molitar, *Tracatus Von Den Bösen Weibern*, 1495.

Bonnie Collura, THE PURSUIT OF HAPPINESS detail, 1999. Collection Oak Park Bank, Chicago.

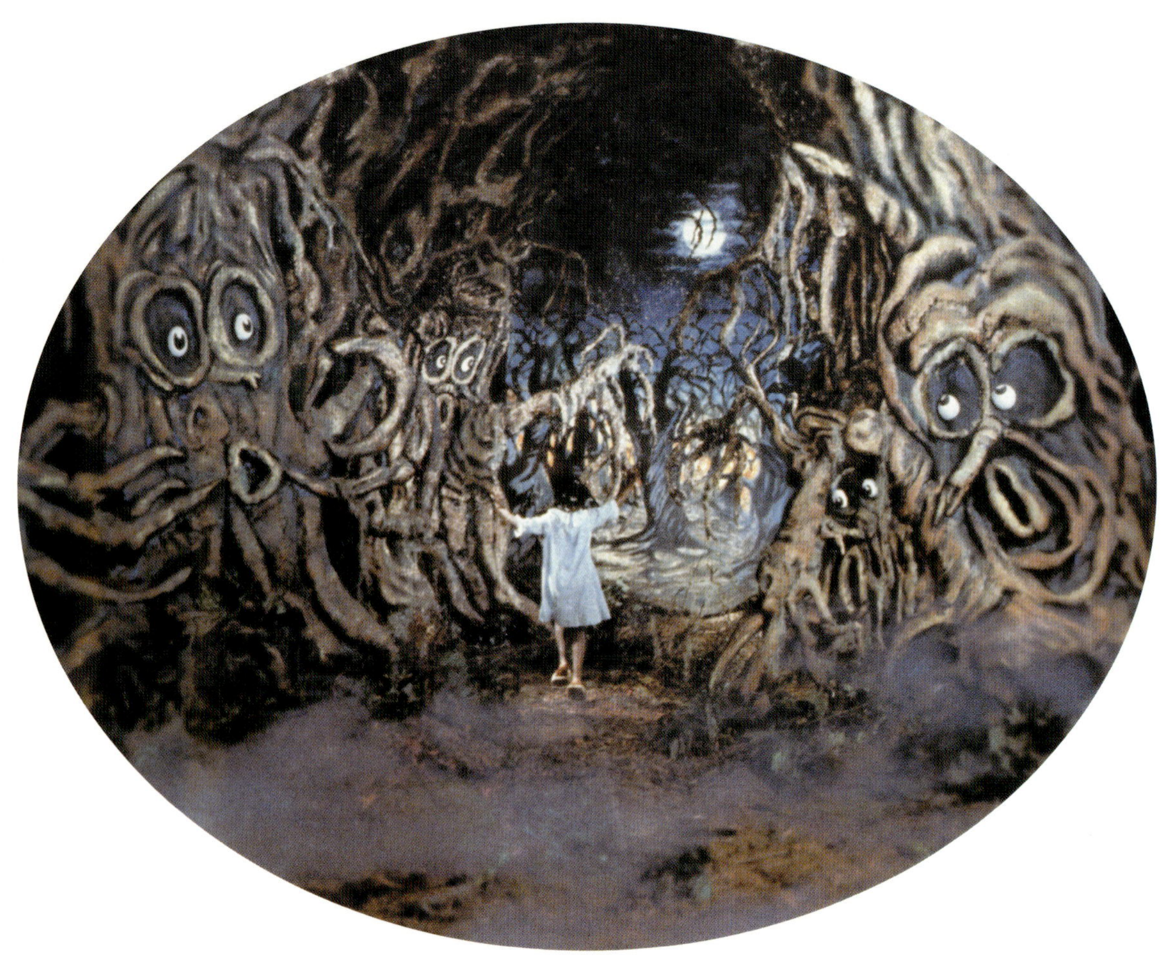

Tracey Moffatt, INVOCATIONS 9, 2000
Photograph and silkscreen on paper, 53 1/2 x 63 inches
Courtesy Matthew Marks Gallery and Paul Morris Gallery, New York
Photo: Karl Rademacher

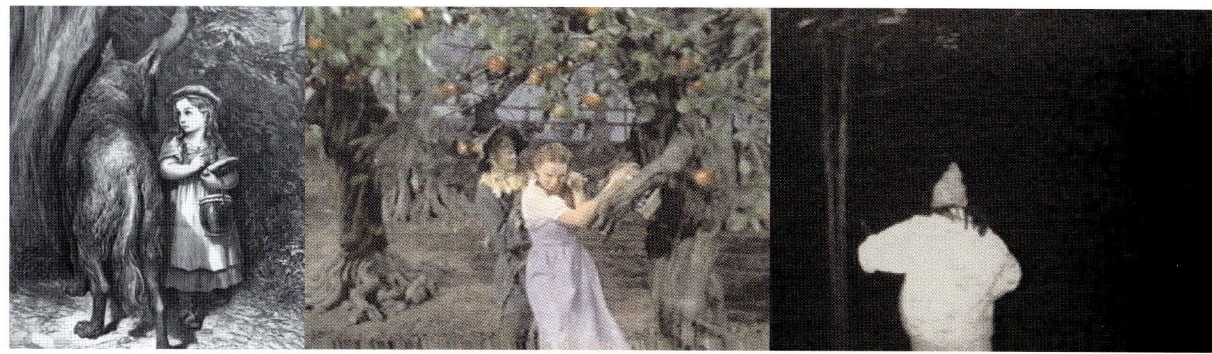

works, twisted echoes of fairy-tale characters are drawn from sampled bits of children's books so old and worn in use and familiarity as to be public domain in more senses than one. The cumulative effect of this quoting and layering is that the familiar is made strange and the unfamiliar is made naggingly common and necessary, like a prince turned into a frog.

Typical of her washy, ethereal worlds in which plant, human and animal forms morph smoothly into each other, foreground each other and stand for each other, Amy Sillman's TREE seems to sprout fleshy pink feet as its trunk and roots drape behind it like a gown. Yellow drops (teardrops, urine, sweat, acid rain, defoliant poison?) fall from the leaves and between the feet, contrasting with the ominous black fruit that the branches bear.

a forest of signs

The forest has historically been a blind spot in our psyche. In the *The Blair Witch Project*, the camera sprints along with the female character, sinking farther and farther into an ocean of night and fear, just as Little Red

Riding Hood, Hansel and Gretel, Dorothy Gale (of Kansas and Oz) and countless others have before her. Our fairy-tale ancestors were more at home in the woods, and so less frightened there (as Stephen King has shown us, even a cornfield can terrify city folks, suddenly in nature, and drowning) than we are. The more cultural we become, the more all of nature frightens us a little.

And sometimes we frighten nature in return. In Tracey Moffatt's INVOCATIONS 9, the Aboriginal heroine runs through a forest of cartoon trees who flail their branches as the mouths on their trunks mimic the letter O. Rather than threatening the young girl, the trees are recoiling in shock and disgust, presumably from the sight of her non-European features. In a twist on Snow White's escape from the Black Forest, her black skin turns the forest white with fear.

strange brew

As if promising miraculous physical improvement and endless youth in a world that has lost its magic, Maria Porges' wax bottles bear gold-leaf inscriptions that allude to magic and metamorphosis, with terms like

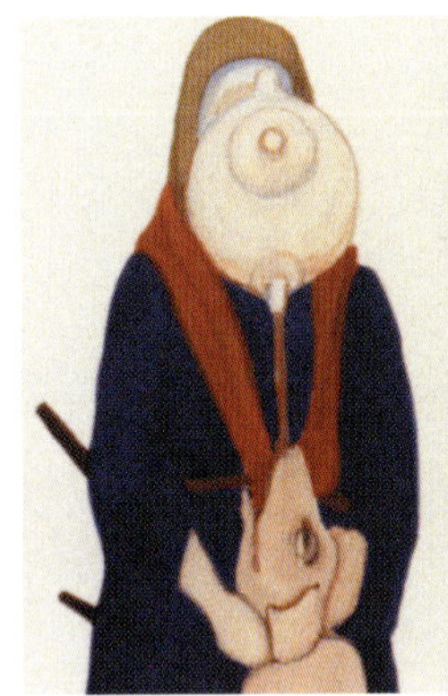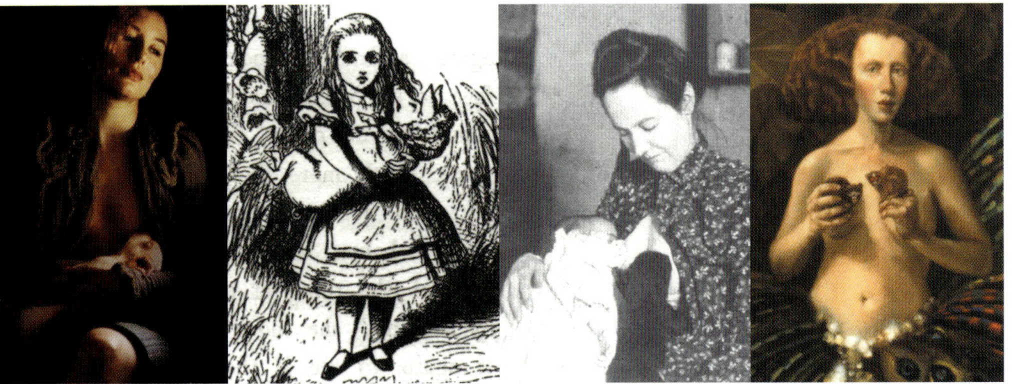

Amy Cutler, EGG COLLECTION detail, 1999. Courtesy Eyewash, Williamsburg.

Photograph of Tori Amos suckling a pig, from the *Boys For Pele* CD. Photo by Cindy Palmano.

John Tenniel, illustration from *Alice's Adventures in Wonderland*.

William Lyman Underwood, photograph from *Wild Brother* showing a woman suckling a baby and bear cub, 1921.

Julie Heffernan, SELF-PORTRAIT AS INFANTA DREAMING MADAME DE SADE detail, 1999. Courtesy P·P·O·W, New York.

"prestidigitation" and "lycanthropy." The implication that these skills and states can be bottled, even in radiantly colored and oddly shaped bottles like these, is part of the magic in this work; another part is the implication it offers that every still life (Cezanne, Morandi and so on) is as much a landscape of ideas as of bottles or fruit, and we can be pretty specific about what the ideas are if we so choose.

The logic that turns boys into frogs and back again turns men into pigs as well. Hilary Harkness' VIEW OF A SLAUGHTERYARD presents a Bosch-like barnyard full of pixie-girls done up like supermodels, ready to turn pigs into sausage. It's a bloody, messy business, and they're certainly not dressed for it, but they're going at it anyway. In the *Malleus Maleficarum* (*The Hammer of Witches*), *1486*, a Catholic and anti-witch book, we are told that "[the] word woman is used to mean lust of the flesh, as it is said: I have found a woman more bitter than death..."[3] Sex? Death? Why certainly, say the Pixies. And will that be one lump or two?

The party continues with Amy Cutler's gouache-on-paper triptych, TEA POT HEAD. Here, the teapot, acting as the artist's surrogate, dons a blue robe in order to impersonate the Virgin Mary. In a collage of myths and roles, the foreshortened top of the teapot becomes a breast pouring fluid (tea or milk?) into the mouth of a pig. So here the Virgin/Child image and the Roman Charity image of daughter and father meet halfway, mediated by the image of Circe and her pigs. The messages here are in two different registers. On the one side, we learn that god is to man as father is to son as man is to pig; and on the other side, we learn that the mediation of these identities is women's work, sometimes performed by virgins, sometimes nymphs, and sometimes witches. And generally, as the signifiers tend to be slippery and messy, a girl has to play all three roles at once, making her costume changes on the fly.

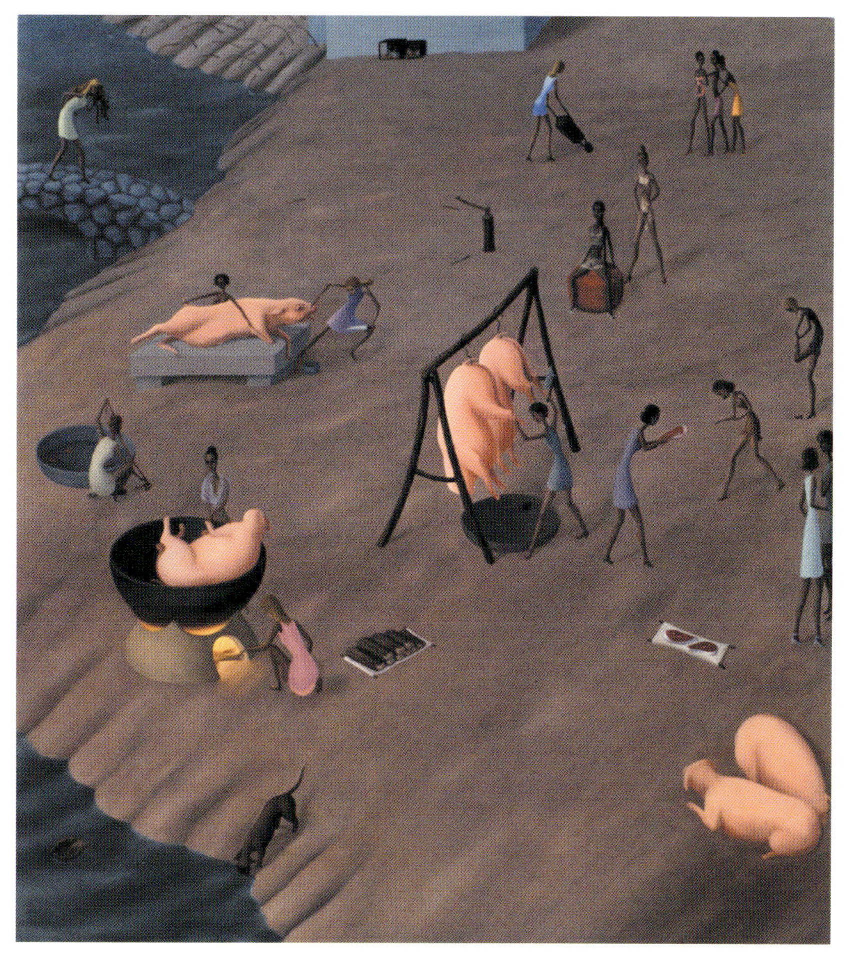

Hilary Harkness, VIEW OF A SLAUGHTER YARD, 2000
Oil on panel, 13 x 11 3/4 inches
Collection Paul Hertz and James Rauchman
Courtesy Bill Maynes Gallery, New York

spindles and pricks

Speaking to girls and their place in a patriarchal world, the many versions of *Little Red Riding Hood* teach them to avoid succumbing to the "wolf." In later versions Red defeats the wolf, killing off the masculine oppressor.[4] So as in many of *pixerina*WITCHERINA's works, symbols of men—in particular the phallus—are rendered inoperative and detached.

The toadstools in Julia Latané's FAIRY RING are prime examples of signifier slippage. This sculpture evokes the stone rings of the pre-celtic ancients (Stonehenge, Avebury and so on) and at the same time draws us back to a more recent Britain—to the vinyl go-go boots, minis, belts and coats once sold on Carnaby Street in Swinging London. Indeed, what is most striking about this circular forest of primary (phallic) signifiers is how unnatural they look, feel, and smell.

Knitting and sewing—while connecting women to story-telling through expressions like "spinning a yarn" and "weaving a plot"—also constituted avenues for art making. Margaret Curtis' BROKEN HORIZON depicts a castrated maypole festooned with shredded remnants of ribbons and picnic plaid, resting on a festering and ravaged earthscape. The torn swatches reveal their making as the paint itself appears to have been woven, simultaneously depicting subject and the rich tradition of its making.

grimm reminders

Claudia Hart constructs a vocabulary out of children's book illustrations, using them as Amy Cutler does, to tell new and disquieting stories. Katharina Fritsch, whose sculptures lift and separate the subjects of cultural obsession (rats, money bags, poodles, virgins) is represented in this show by a loop of layered sounds: an ambulance (*ein Krankenwagen*), thunder, and spring peepers.

Karen Arm's paintings aren't so much depictions as alchemical abstractions—distillations of natural phenomena that

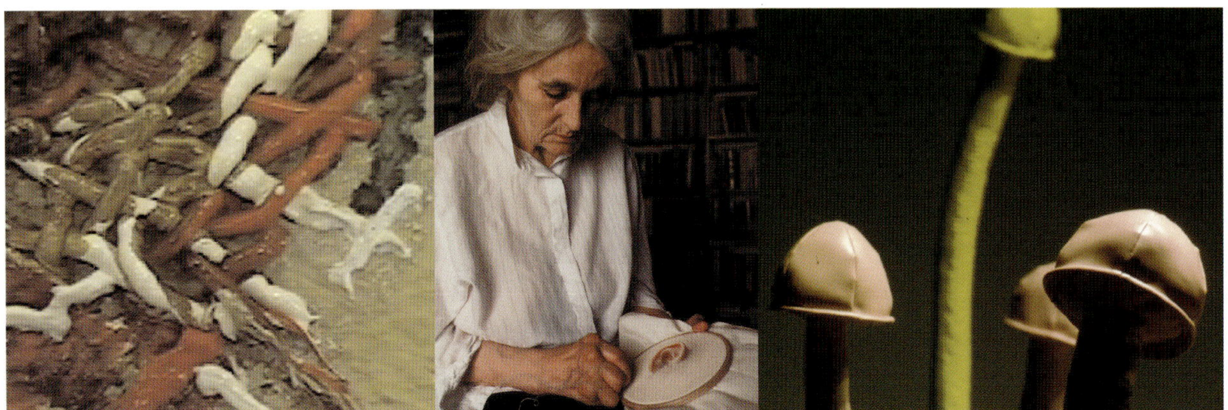

Margaret Curtis, BROKEN HORIZON detail, 1998. Courtesy P·P·O·W, New York.

Margi Geerlinks, UNTITLED detail, 1999. Courtesy Stefan Stux Gallery, New York.

Julia Latané, FAIRY RING detail. 1999. Courtesy the artist.

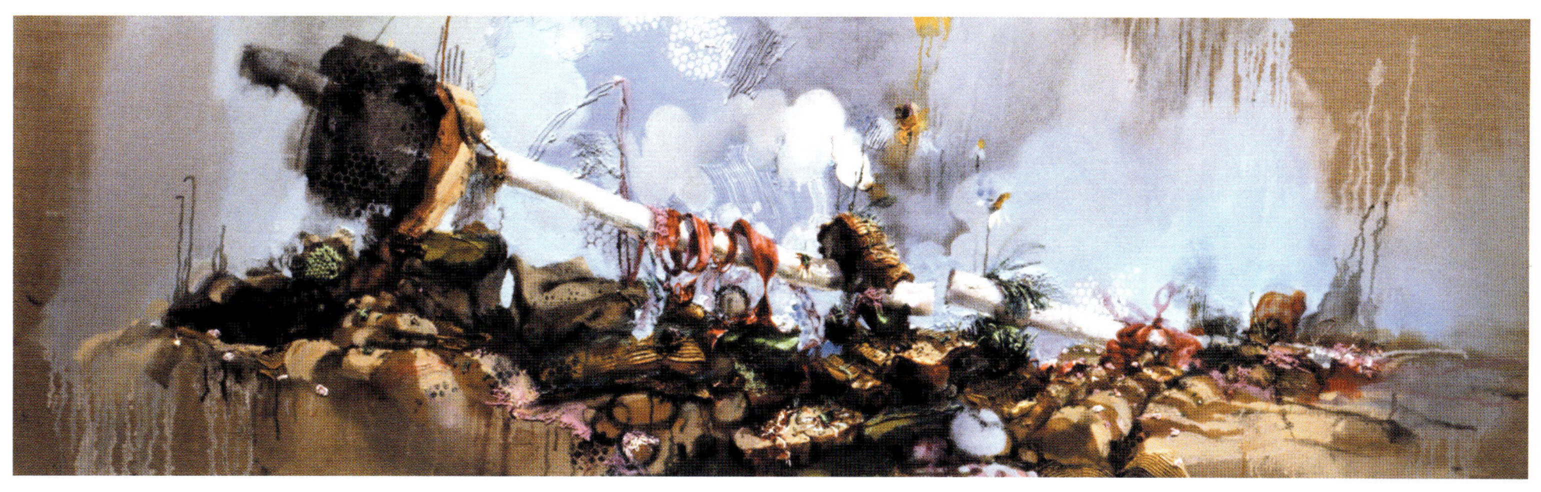

Margaret Curtis, BROKEN HORIZON, 1998
Oil on linen, 24 x 80 inches
Courtesy P·P·O·W, New York
Photo: Karl Rademacher

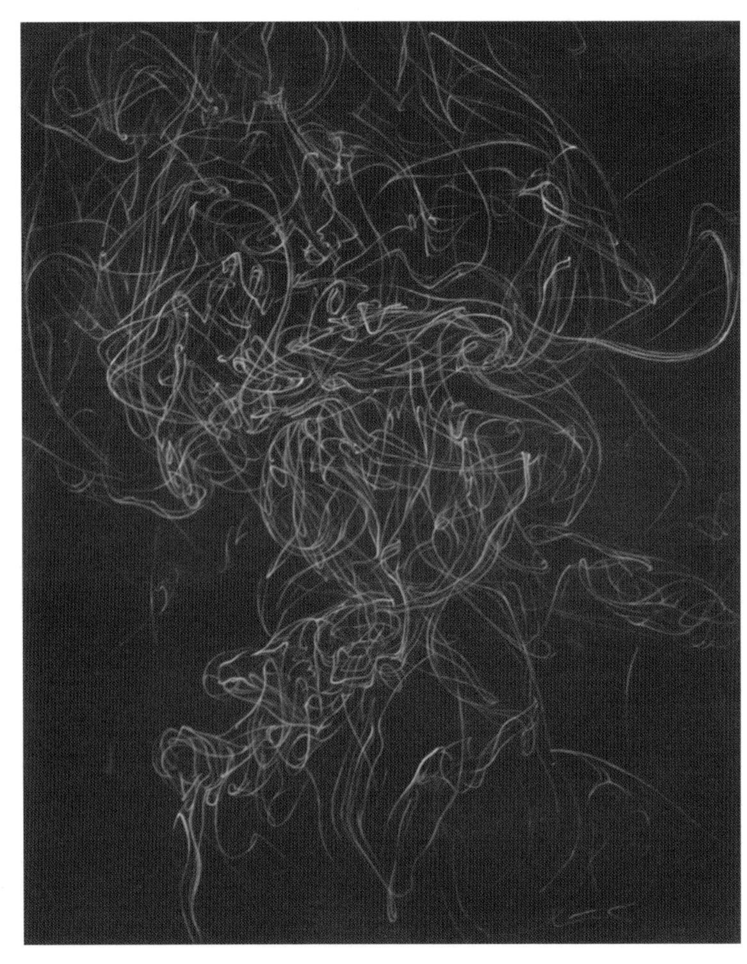

Karen Arm, SMOKE DRAWING # 5, 2000
Acrylic on paper, 20 x 17 inches
Courtesy P·P·O·W, New York

become, in use, indexical emblems of folk narrative, like smoke wisps, blood droplets, tree roots, fire and water.

Elena Sisto is willing to populate her paintings with monsters like NOGUE. Even her Snow White has a sickened, tired quality. Being good has been such a strain. The evil these paintings represent runs the full range from the dreadful (like Goya's child-eating Saturn, NOGUE is as ugly as she needs to be to inhabit her role in life) to the dreadfully ordinary. Back in the Old Europe in which Johann Haizmann[5] painted highly encoded images of the devil which he believed his father to be, they didn't yet believe that evil was or could be banal, or that fascism was sexy. The monsters who emerge from the dark to rip our lives apart for casual fun are now, as then, male (Dahmer, Gacy, Bundy), but part of the premise for these painters, as well as this exhibit in general, is that women (as Pixies or as Witches, operating under the cover of the Old Faith) can be as "evil" as anyone could imagine being.

The corny, binary image of women as moral and cultural operators (Madonna/whore, Betty/Veronica) is a lacework of blind spots, but the one spot that stands out, and is the primary topic of this show, is that moment at the end of childhood and the beginning of something else that Nabokov and Balthus have staked out as a personal reserve, and that deserves something better. The images in *pixerina*WITCHERINA are wrested away from the gritty past of folktale and its current Disnification, but the new context which these artists are creating has another task as well, a kind of declaration of independence.

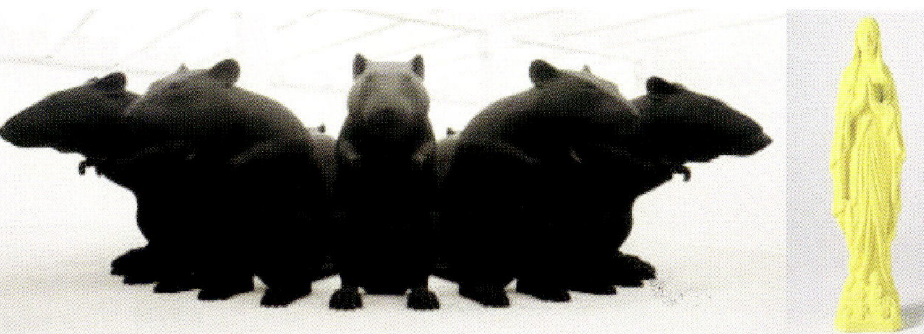

Katharina Fritsch, *Rat King (Rattenkönig)*, 1993. Installation at Dia Art Center, New York.

Katharina Fritsch, *Madonna (Madonnenfigur)*, 1982. Collection of Walker Art Center, Minneapolis.

Francisco Goya, *Saturn Devouring His Sons* (detail), c. 1821 - 23 Museo Del Prado, Madrid.

An apparition of Satan painted by Johann Haizmann, 1677.

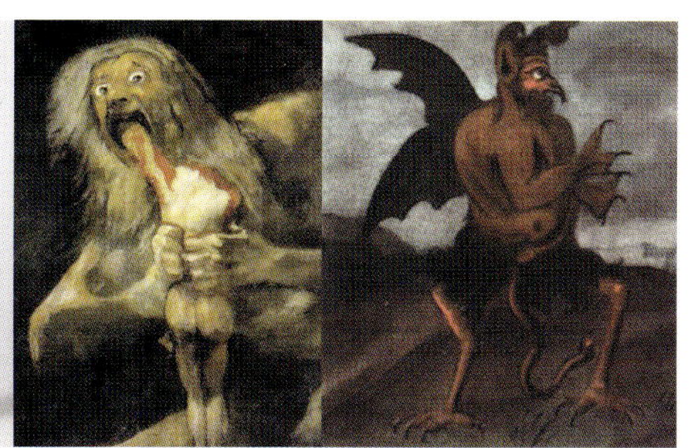

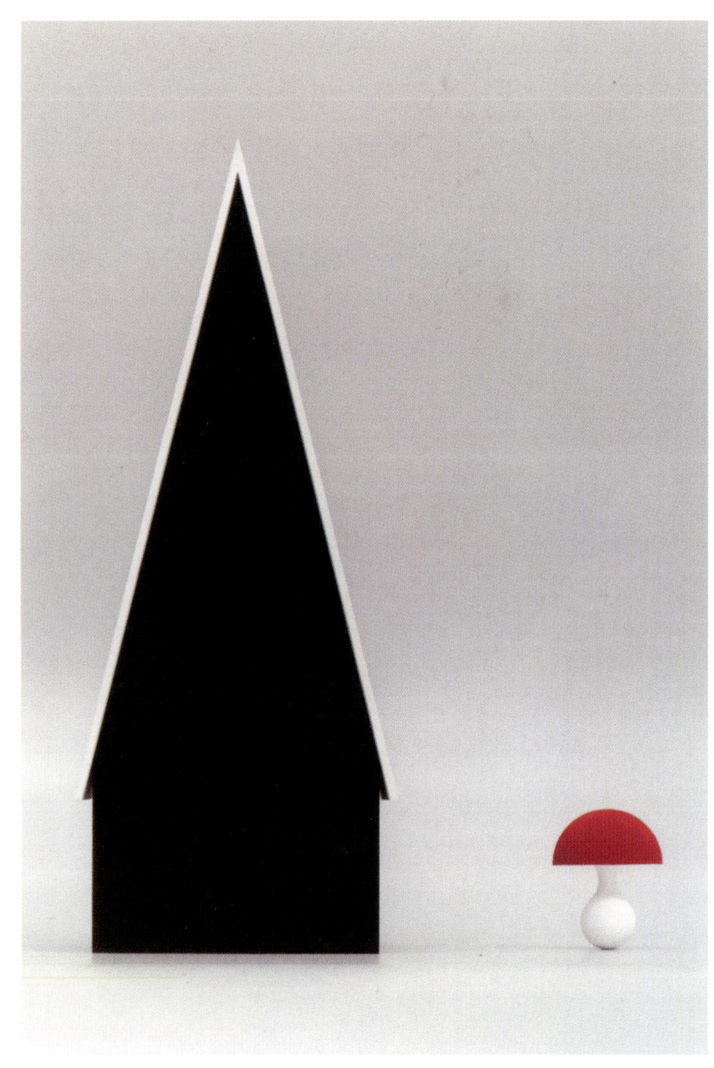

Katharina Fritsch, HEXENHAUS UND PILZ (WITCHHOUSE AND MUSHROOM), 1999
Wood and acrylic paint, 31 x 15 3/4 x 15 3/4 inches and 6 x 4 3/4 x 4 3/4 inches
Photo courtesy Matthew Marks Gallery, New York

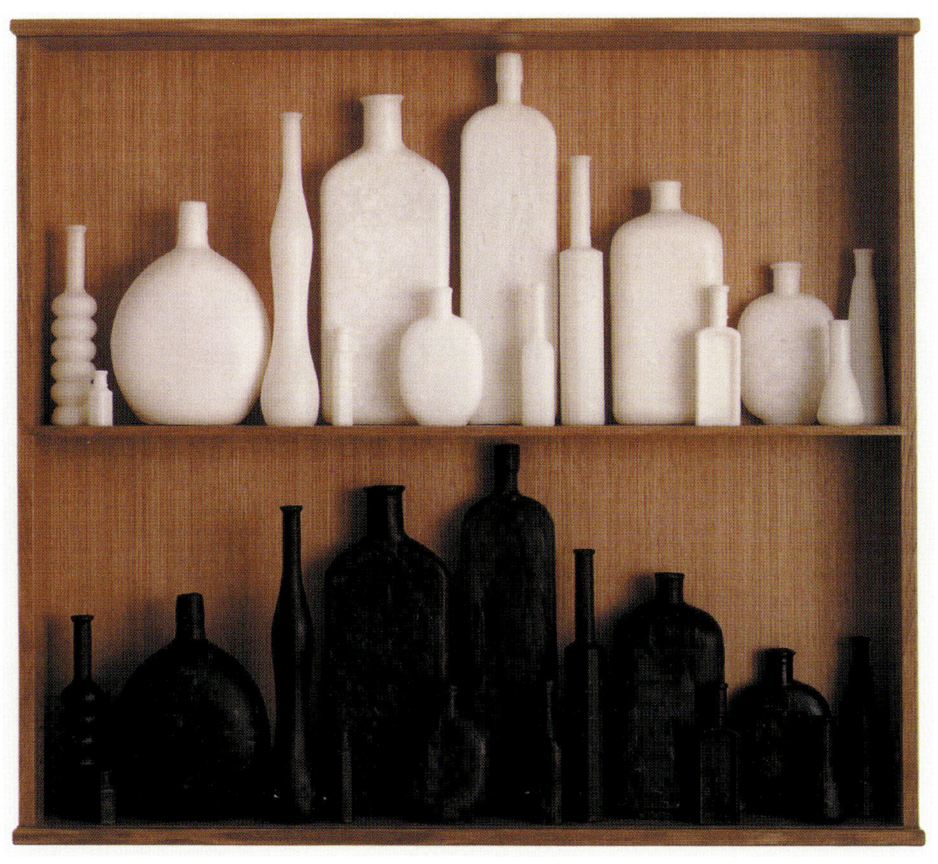

Maria Porges, BLACK & WHITE MAGIC FOR CLAUDE LEVI-STRAUSS, 2000
Wax, wood, and applied text, 31 3/4 x 36 1/2 inches
Courtesy John Berggruen Gallery, San Francisco

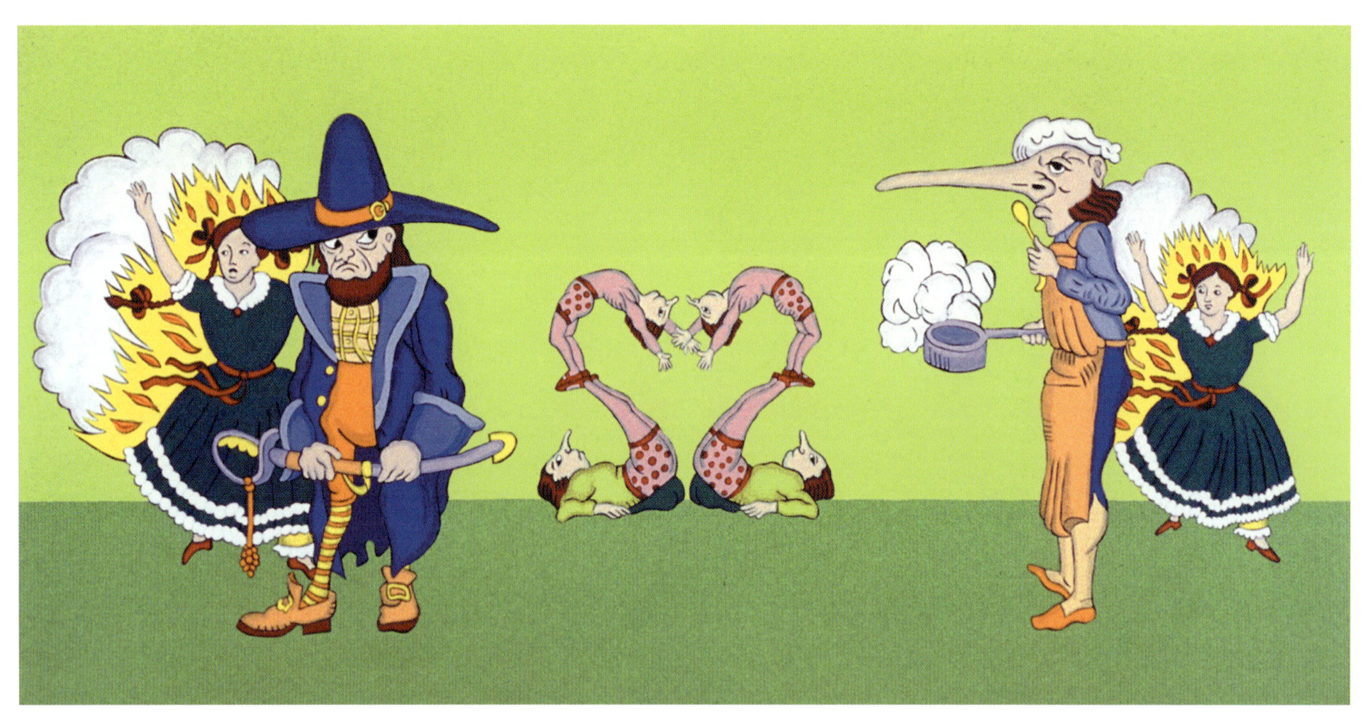

Claudia Hart, A LOVE STORY INVOLVING TWO GUYS, 1998
Acrylic on canvas, 30 x 60 inches
Courtesy Sandra Gering Gallery, New York

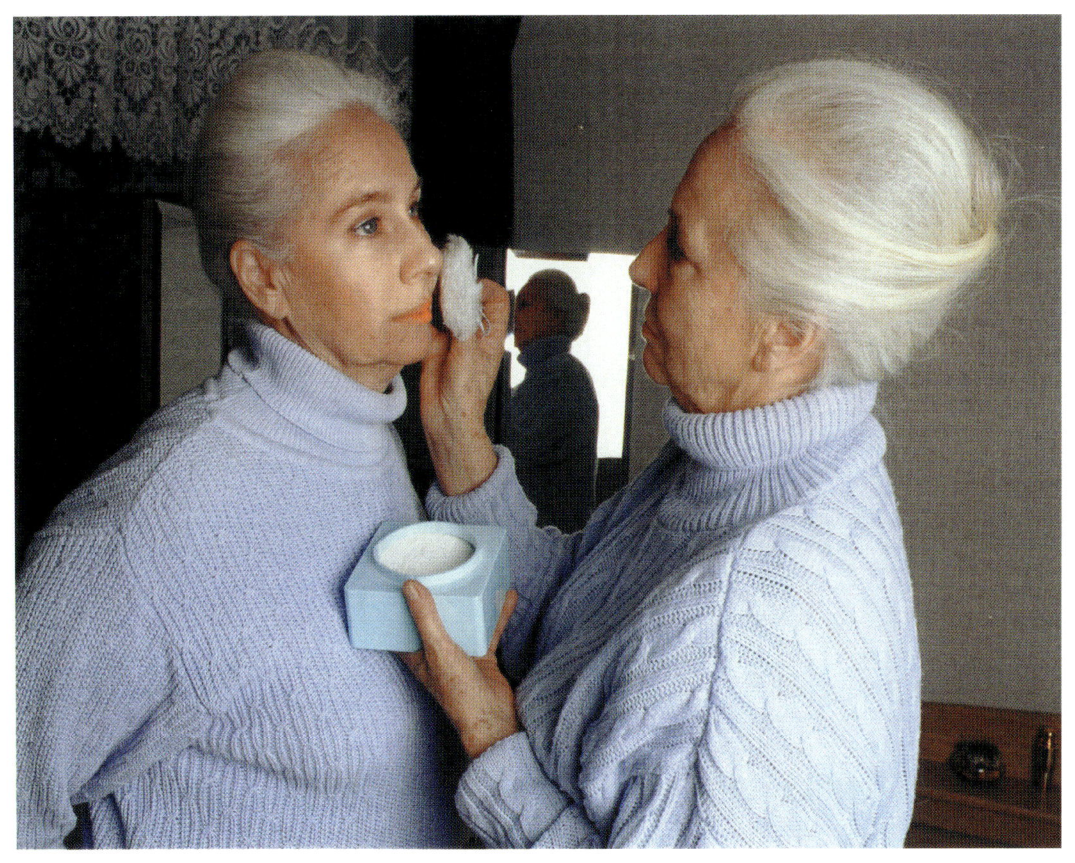

Margi Geerlinks, UNITITLED (TWINS), 1999
Fujichrome, perspex, and dibond, 49 1/4 x 60 inches
Courtesy Stefan Stux Gallery, New York

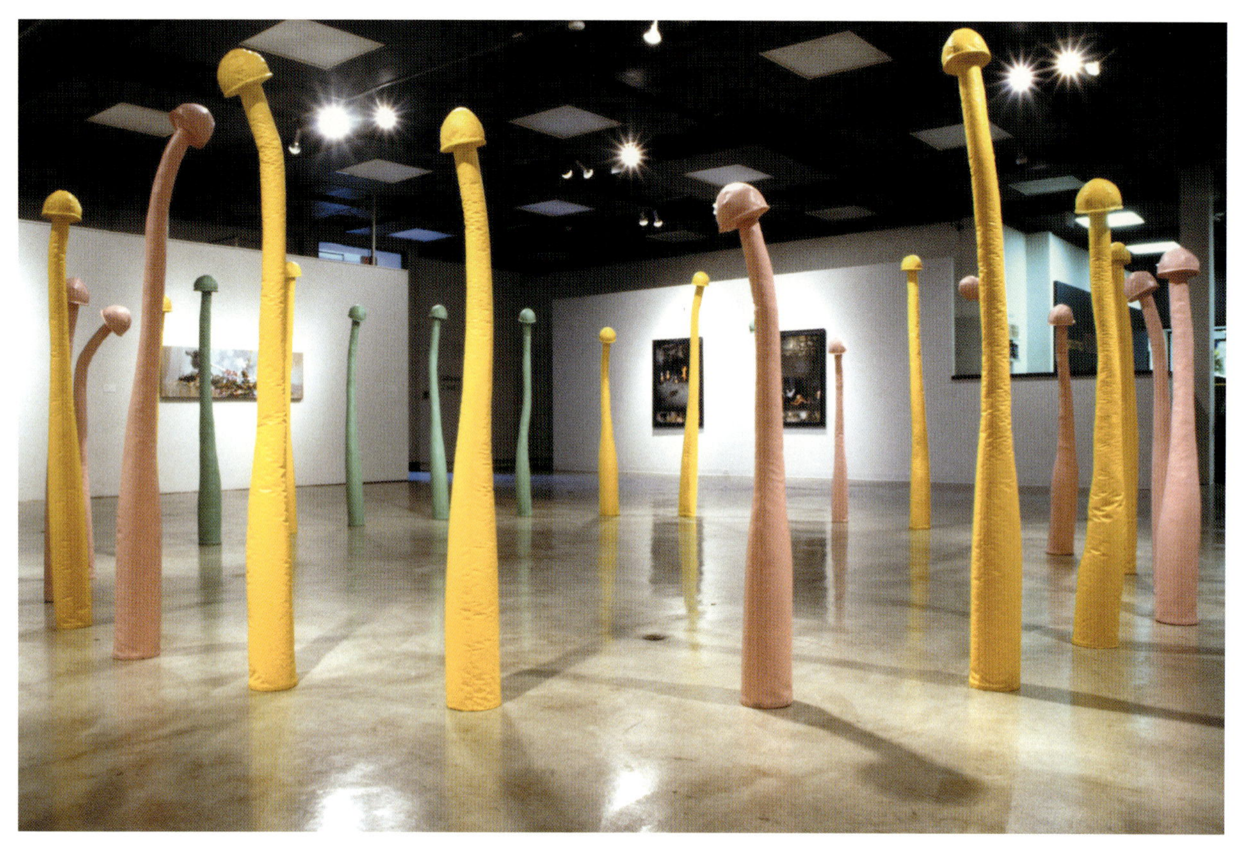

Julia Latané, *FAIRY RING*, 1999
Installation at University Galleries, 2001
Vinyl, 192 x 192 x 84 inches
Courtesy the artist
Photo: Karl Rademacher

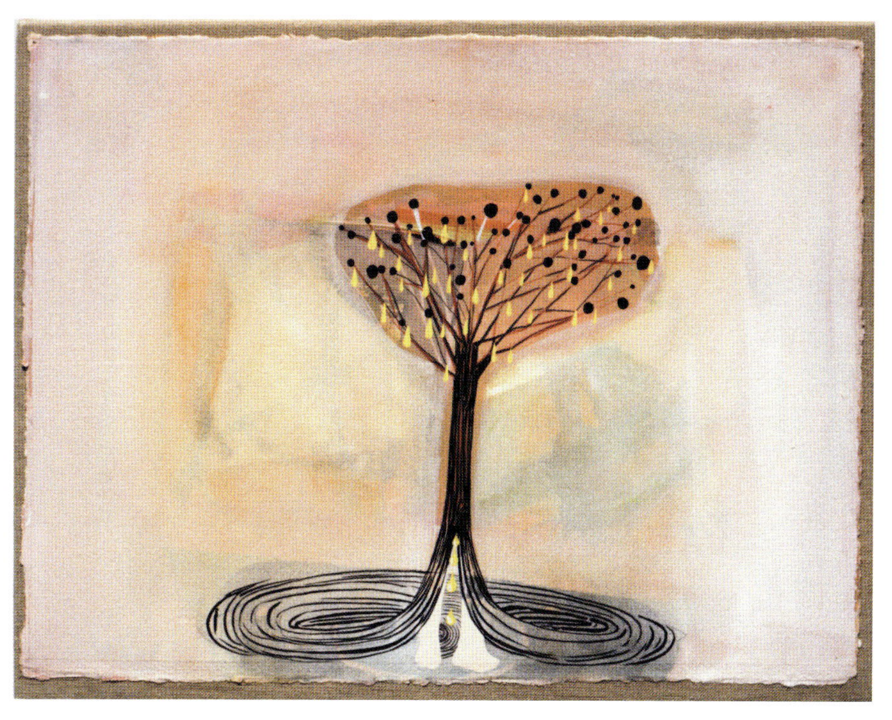

Amy Sillman, TREE. 1999
Watercolor and gouache on paper mounted on linen, 12 x 15 1/2 inches
Courtesy Brent Sikkema Gallery, New York
Photo: Karl Rademacher

INVOCATIONS OF FAIRY TALES

Maria Tatar

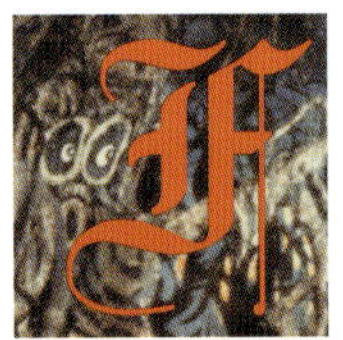

Fairy tales are up close and personal, telling us about the quest for romance and riches, for power and privilege, and, most importantly, for a way out of the woods, back to the safety and security of home. Bringing myths down to earth and inflecting them in human rather than heroic terms, fairy tales put a familiar spin on the stories in the archive of our collective imagination. Think of Petit Poucet, who miniaturizes David's killing of Goliath, Odysseus's blinding of Polyphemus, and Siegfried's conquest of Fafner. Or consider Cinderella, who is sister under the skin to Shakespeare's Cordelia and to Brontë's Jane Eyre. Fairy tales take us into a reality that is familiar in the double sense of the term—deeply personal and at the same time centered on the family and its conflicts rather than on what is at stake in the world at large.

That many of the stories recorded by Perrault and, a century later, by the Brothers Grimm had their origins in an adult culture becomes evident from the preoccupations and ambitions of the key figures. Perrault's Sleeping Beauty may act like a careless, disobedient child when she reaches for the spindle that puts her to sleep, but her real troubles come in the form of a hostile mother-in-law who plans to serve her for dinner with a sauce Robert. "Bluebeard," with its forbidden chamber filled with the corpses of former wives, engages with issues of marital trust, fidelity, and betrayal, showing how marriage is haunted by the threat of murder. "Rumpelstiltskin" charts a woman's narrow escape from a bargain that could cost the life of her firstborn. "Rapunzel" turns on the perilous cravings of pregnant woman and on the impossibility of safeguarding a daughter's virtue by locking her up in a tower.

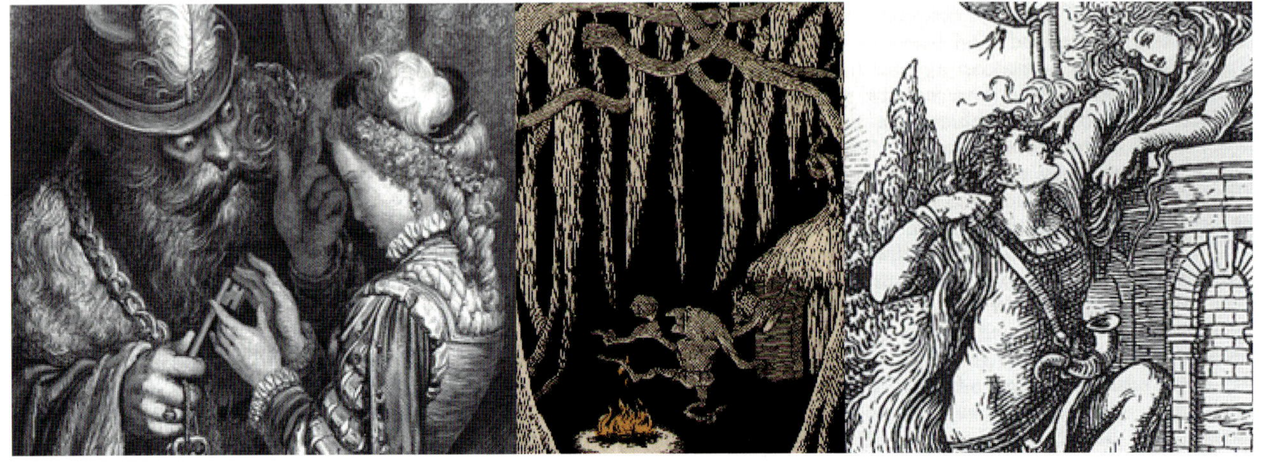

Gustave Doré, illustration detail for Charles Perrault's *Bluebeard*, 1862.

Edward Gorey, illustration detail from *Rumpelstiltskin*, 1973.

Walter Crane, illustration detail from "Rapunzel" from *Household Stories by the Brothers Grimm*, 1886.

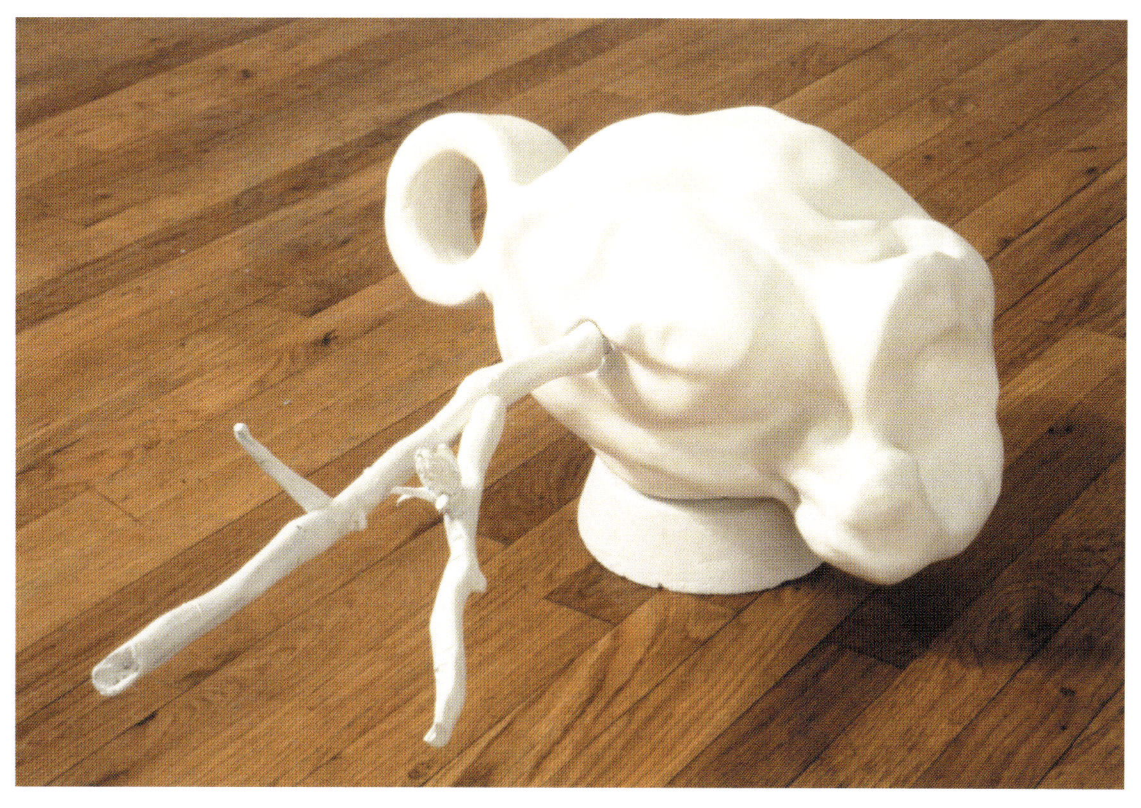

Bonnie Collura, BERNINI'S PERSEPHONE (CRONE), 1997
Plaster gauzing and foam, 10½ x 18 inches
Courtesy Lehmann Maupin Gallery, New York

John Updike reminds us that fairy tales were "the television and pornography of their day, the life-lightening trash of preliterate peoples." (Updike 662). Once told by peasants around the fireside to distract them from the tedium of repairing tools, mending clothes, or kneading dough, they have now been successfully transplanted into the nursery for the entertainment and edification of children. Many of these tales, filled with bawdy turns of phrase and off-color humor, were not intended for children's ears, though children were often in attendance when folk raconteurs spun their tales. And while the melodramatic plots and burlesque flourishes of those tales may once have captured the attention of children, the actual plots rarely accorded with the anxieties and desires of pre-adolescents, who were surely more interested in getting their next meal or in evading a chore than in marital matters.

If the matter of the old fairy tales has moved to the nursery, the manner of tale-telling remains, mutatis mutandi, very much alive in adult culture. In the form of gossip, jokes, rumor, scandal, and news, we continue to blend the real with the surreal, to mingle whimsy with truth, and to mix sober fact with burlesque fiction. Stories are our social and cultural capital, circulating among us in powerful ways and ensuring that we have ways of talking about our fantasies and anxieties, about what we value and cherish as well as what we hate and deplore.

With conspiratorial pleasure, the narrator of Margaret Atwood's "Significant Moments in the Life of My Mother" reports that there are always "some stories which my mother does not tell when there are men present: never at dinner, never at parties." These stories, we learn, are told in domestic settings: "usually in the kitchen, when they or we are helping with the dishes or shelling peas, or taking the tops and tails off the string beans, or husking corn." They are melodramatic tales, charting the consequences of "romantic betrayals, unwanted pregnancies, illnesses of various horrible kinds, marital infidelities, mental breakdowns, tragic suicides, unpleasant lingering deaths." Like the spirited tales once spun around the fireside, these stories are "not rich in detail or embroidered with incident: they are stark and factual." They encapsulate collective truths—the wisdom of the ages—about romance, courtship, marriage, divorce, and death, and they are passed on from one generation of women to the next. Gossip and gospel truth, gossip as gospel truth, these stories are received with reverent attention: "The women, their own hands moving among the dirty dishes or the husks of vegetables, nod solemnly." (Atwood 14-15).

The old wives' tales to which Atwood is referring continue a narrative tradition, one that has flowed largely through oral tributaries as women's speech. It is fluid, mercurial, and volatile, unlike the fairy tales that were channeled into a print culture. Atwood's observations about her childhood suggest that this oral tradition remains very much alive today, drawing its strength from the lived experience of women and existing side by side with a literary tradition that records historical experience in the form of story.

As the cultural critic Marina Warner has pointed out, the tales told by Atwood's mother and by her friends have a vital social function. Their power is trained not only on adult listeners but also on small children, who, like Margaret Atwood in her youth, are positioned on the margins of the storyteller's circle. Conveying social attitudes and expectations, the tellers of tales "pass on vital information about the values and beliefs of the community in which they are growing up, will instruct them in who is trusted and who is not, about what is considered praiseworthy and what is condemned, about alliances and enmities, hopes and dangers." The stories they tell map out different developmental trajectories: "They chart the terrain. Some directions are urged, but the signposts are not entirely coercive. Gossip and narrative are sisters, both ways of keeping the mind alive when ordinary tasks call; the fictions of gossip—as well as the facts—act as compass roses, pointing to many possibilities" (Warner 1994, 49).

Today fairy tales thrive in two very different cultural regimes. On the one hand, we have the literary tradition, a powerful folklore that has, for the most part, migrated into the nursery in the form of the monumental national collections from earlier centuries, of the many stories reissued, adapted, and retold, and of the subtle appropri-ations of fairy-tale plots. There is another archive as well, one that is not written in granite or even on the pages of books, but that exists as a kind of collective cultural unconscious. Many of these are versions of the fairy tales in books, but in a more elastic form, supple enough to be invoked as we try to understand daily experience and to work through events. With the help of those stories, we navigate daily experience, making sense of it, interpreting it, digesting it, and producing the kinds of narratives Margaret Atwood heard in her mother's kitchen. Just as proverbs offer help on how to size up a situation—telling us how to cope with perils and how to stand up to adversity—fairy tales can provide readers and listeners with counsel about how to manage anxieties that run particularly deep. How many times do we invoke "Cinderella" when it comes to thinking about courtship, marriage, and romance? How often do we think of "Little Red Riding Hood" when a vulnerable young innocent is pitted against a predator? And how frequently do we frame marriages as repetitions of "Beauty and the Beast"? That writers, filmmakers, and artists constantly recycle these stories reveals the degree to which they are perpetually in the back of our collective minds.

While some of these stories address primal anxieties of childhood, others are attuned to fantasies about what happens after we leave home, about the adult themes to which I referred. *pixerina*WITCHERINA evokes images that resonate powerfully with those anxieties and fantasies. I

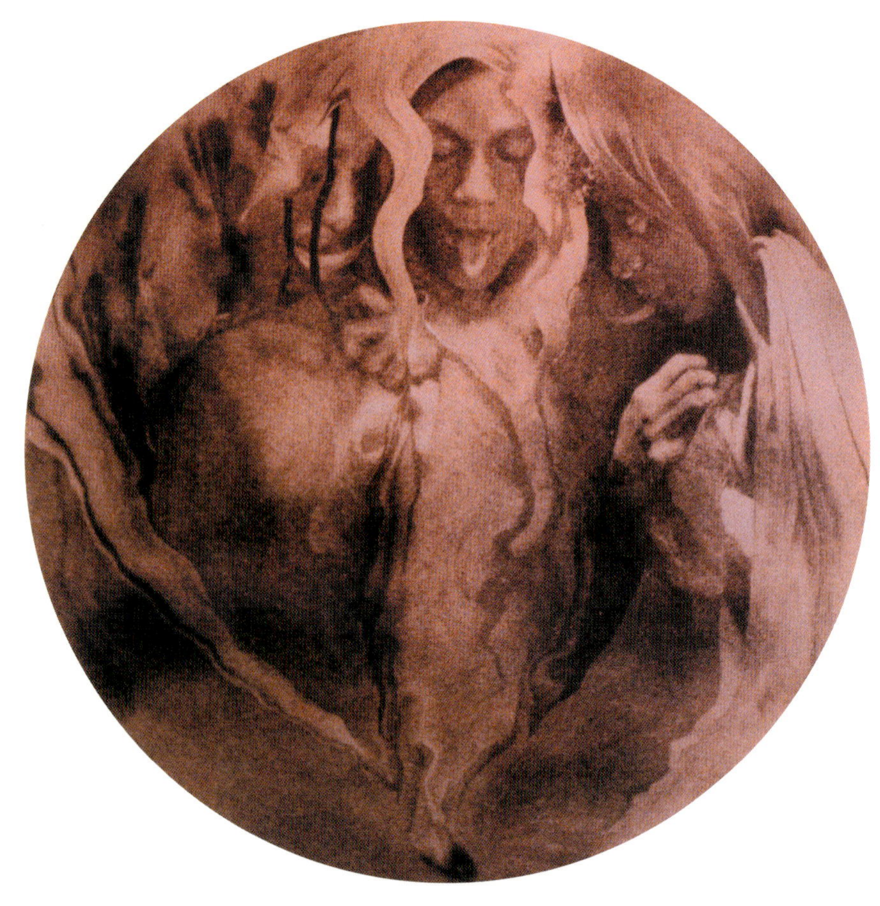

Tracey Moffatt, INVOCATIONS #13, 2000
Photograph and silkscreen on paper, 48 1/2 x 43 1/2 inches
Courtesy Matthew Marks Gallery and Paul Morris Gallery, New York
Photo: Karl Rademacher

want to use some of those images as a springboard for thinking about the wonders of fairy tales, for reflecting on the way in which a single picture can evoke the thousand words of a story in our collective cultural archive.

's INVOCATIONS 3 gives us a house in the woods. It may not be the gingerbread house of the wicked witch, the cozy cottage of the three bears, or the home of the seven dwarfs, but it draws on the power of the house in all those stories to produce its effect. As we look at the light in the window, we are positioned as the lost child of fairy tale, abandoned by parents and seeking a way out of the woods.

What story evokes more powerful emotions than the tale of Hansel and Gretel, left to starve and unable to find a way back home? "Hansel and Gretel" is a story that celebrates the triumph of children over hostile and predatory adults. Addressing anxieties about abandonment, starvation, and being devoured, it shows two young siblings joining forces to defeat monsters at home and in the woods. Folklorists refer to this and other stories pitting young, powerless protagonists against cruel brutes as "The Children and the Ogre." A child or a group of children innocently enter the abode of an ogre, wicked witch, giant, or other type of villain, succeed in turning the tables on a bloodthirsty antagonist, and flee, often with material goods in the form of jewels or gold.

Sibling solidarity is so rare in fairy tales (think of those evil stepsisters in "Cinderella") that "Hansel and Gretel" provides a unique opportunity for displaying the advantages

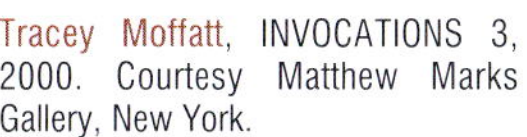

Tracey Moffatt, INVOCATIONS 3, 2000. Courtesy Matthew Marks Gallery, New York.

Gustave Dore, illustration from Charles Perrault's "Hop O' My Thumb," 1862.

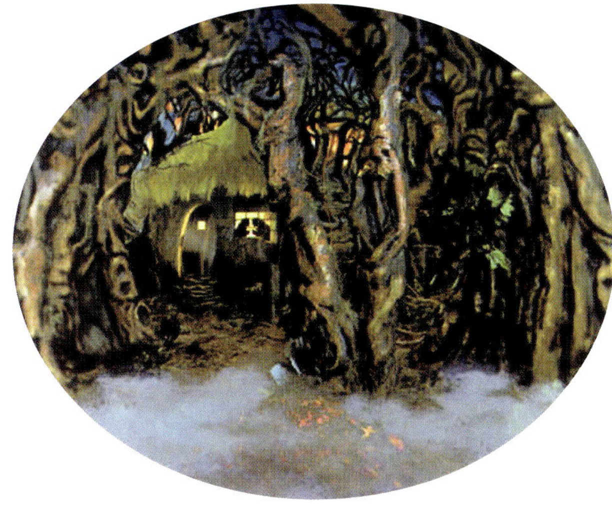

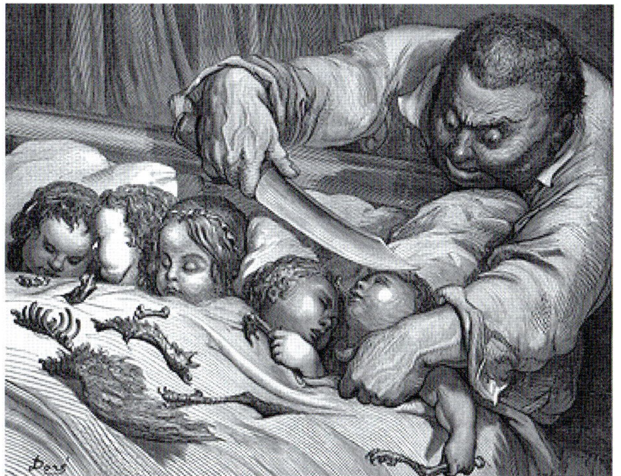

of cooperation between brother and sister. While Hansel takes the lead at the beginning of the tale, soothing Gretel's fears and using his wits to find a way back home, Gretel outsmarts the witch, tricking her into entering the oven. By nineteenth-century standards, the children in "Hansel and Gretel" are youthful insurgents, eavesdropping on their parents' nighttime conversations, deploying a ruse to get back home, greedily feasting on the house of the witch, and running off with the witch's jewels after Gretel pushes her into the oven. Determined to find a way back home, Hansel and Gretel survive what children fear more than anything else: abandonment by parents and exposure to predators.

The story of "Hansel and Gretel," like the mysterious house in the woods with a light in its window, offers a ray of hope. It conveys the lesson that the German philosopher Walter Benjamin saw as the great legacy of the fairy tale: "The wisest thing—so the fairy tale taught mankind in olden times, and teaches children to this day—is to meet the forces of the mythical world with cunning and with high spirits" (102). Is it any wonder that our culture's cinematic fantasies draw on stories like "Hansel and Gretel" to create their popular appeal. From *Jurassic Park*, with its sibling team trapped in the kitchen with deadly female velociraptors, to the mecha Michael, abandoned in the woods by his "mother," in *A.I.*, Hollywood cinema replays stories that for centuries have haunted the western imagination, helping us to work through anxieties and discover that there is a light in the window, even if at first it offers a false promise of hope, bringing to the door the witch that we see in Katharina Fritsch's LEXICON SERIES HANSEL AND GRETEL.

Consider another pair of images: the faces of two women: one an untitled photographic image by Margi Geerlinks, the other Elena Sisto's oil painting of Snow White. One gives us an image that connects powerfully with the fairy-tale fantasy of the fair-haired beauty, a figure who is fully incarnated in Mme d'Aulnoy's "Beauty with the Golden Hair":

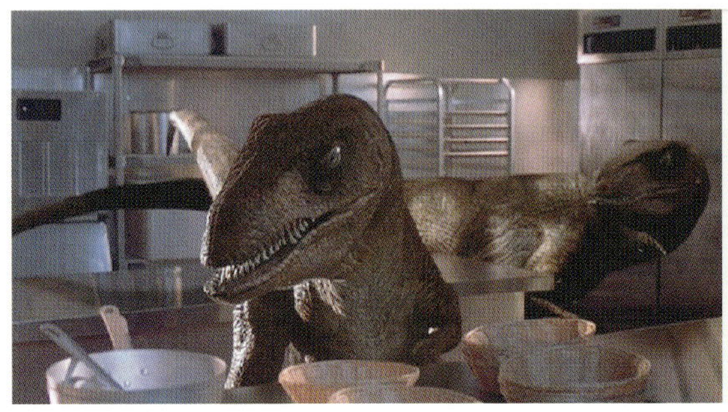

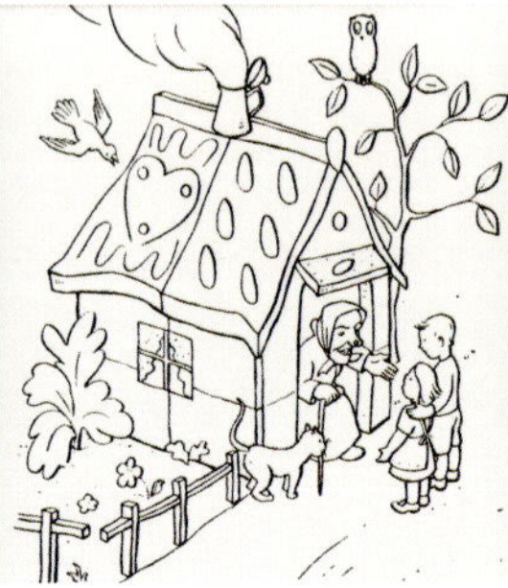

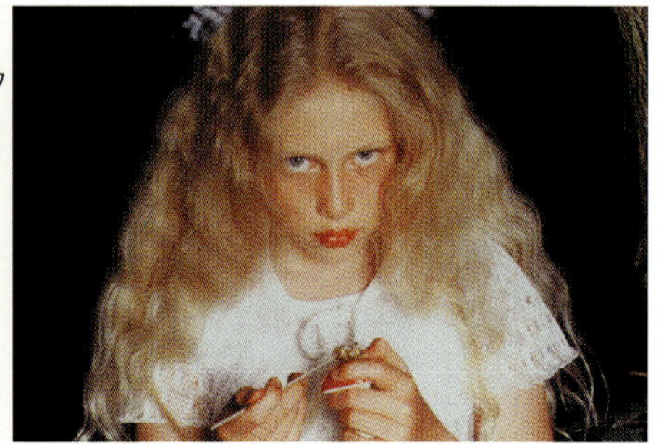

Raptors in the kitchen. Still from *Jurassic Park*, 1993.

Katharina Fritsch, from THE LEXICON SERIES, 1996. Courtesy Matthew Marks Gallery, New York.

Margi Geerlinks, UNTITLED (GIRL) detail, 1999. Courtesy Stefan Stux Gallery, New York.

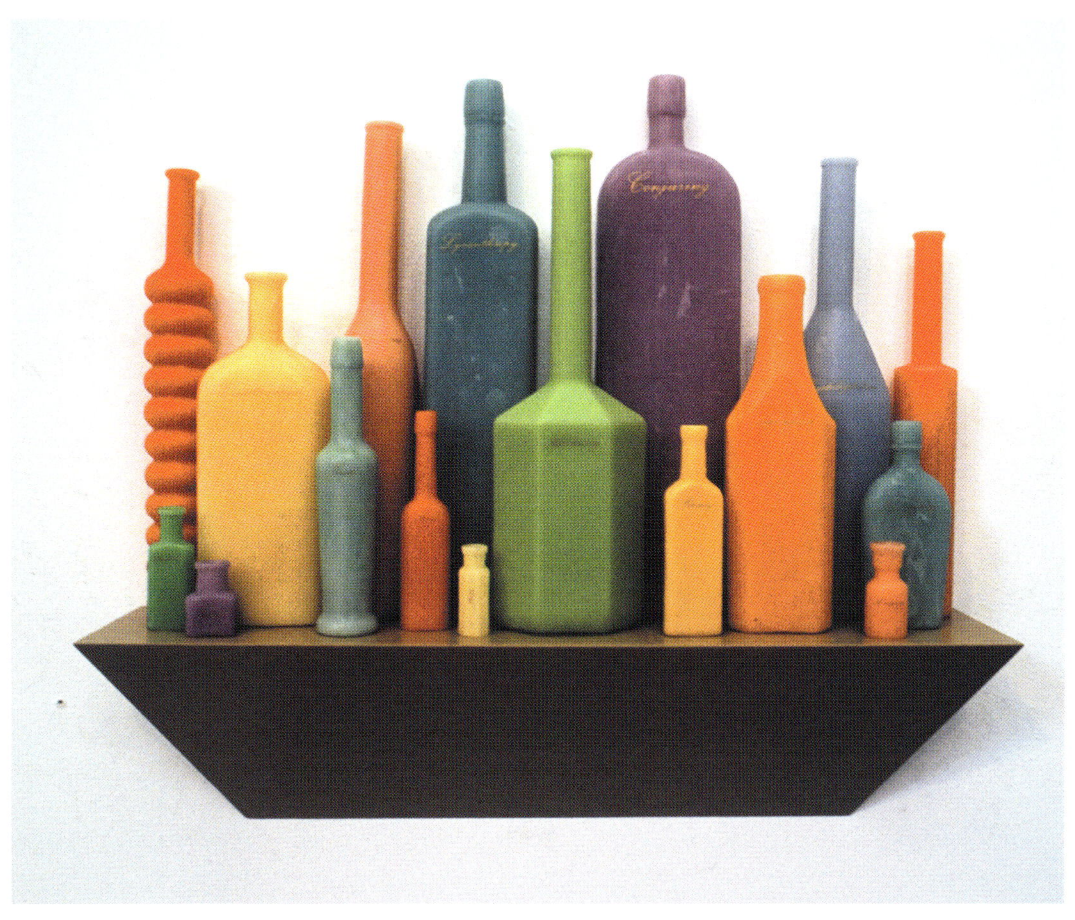

Maria Porges, NAMES OF MAGIC 3, 2000
Wood, beeswax, and applied text, 21 x 24 x 6 inches
Courtesy David Beitzel Gallery and the artist

Once upon a time there lived a princess who was more beautiful than anyone in the world, and she was called Beauty with the Golden Hair, because her locks were radiant like the finest gold and fell in ringlets to her feet. She always appeared with her hair flowing in curls and crowned with flowers, and her dresses were embroidered with diamonds and pearls. It was impossible to look upon her without adoring her. (Zipes 309)

It did not take Walt Disney to establish a connection between blondeness and beauty. Long before Disney Studio began to translate fairy tales to the screen, fairness was a guarantee of purity, goodness, and beauty. Marina Warner emphasizes that it was "a guarantee of quality" and the "opposite of 'foul.'" She notes that "blondeness is less a descriptive term about hair pigmentation than a blazon in code, a piece of a value system that it is urgent to confront and analyze because its implications, in moral and social terms, are so dire and are still so unthinkingly embedded in the most ordinary, popular materials of the imagination" (362). The tresses that tumble down the tower in "Rapunzel" are invariably golden. Cinderella is blonde, while her stepsisters are red-headed and dark-haired, and her stepmother is raven-haired. The golden hair of the Grimms' "All-Fur" is what makes her especially attractive and singles her out from all those around her. Snow White may seem to be the exception that proves the rule, but Snow White's hair color is determined by the mother's wish for a child "white as snow, red as blood, and black as the wood of the window frame." And Snow White, like her fairy-tale cousins, remains a fair heroine by virtue of her skin, which is "white as snow."

If Margi Geerlinks captures the element of the real in fairy-tale fantasies through her photograph, Elena Sisto reveals the reality underlying the fairy-tale fantasy. The fairest of them all, Snow White is not necessarily "white as snow." Rather than conforming to the stereotypes produced by our ancestors, Sisto contests them, reflecting instead on the social realities of a global culture. Today, for example, when we decide to read *Cinderella* to our children, we can choose among a variety of possibilities: there is Jewell Reinhart Coburn's *Cambodian Cinderella*, Shirley Climo's *Persian Cinderella*, Penny Pollock's *Zuni Cinderella*, Jude Daly's *Fair, Brown and Trembling : An Irish Cinderella Story*, in addition to the traditional Cinderellas of Charles Perrault and the Brothers Grimm. Or we can read the stepmother's version of events in Russell Shorto's *Untold Story of Cinderella* or contemplate Roberto Innocenti's unsettling images in *Cinderella : A Creative Tale from the Collection Once upon a Time*. Just as Geerlinks' photograph coexists with Sisto's painting, the fantasies shaped by fairy tales from another time and place manage to thrive alongside those inspired by our contemporary rescriptings.

The new images and words generated by the old tales represent the same kind of hope that we see in the lighted window of Moffat's INVOCATIONS 3. That Sisto's

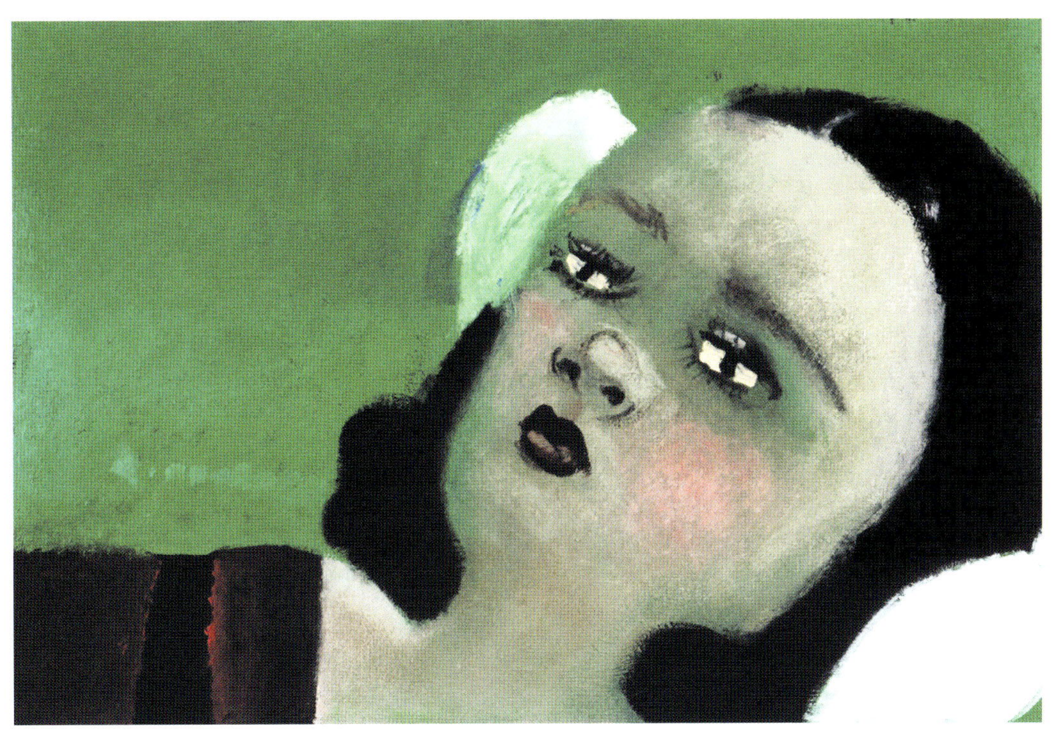

Elena Sisto, SNOW WHITE, 1998
Oil on linen, 24 x 36 inches
Courtesy Littlejohn Contemporary, New York

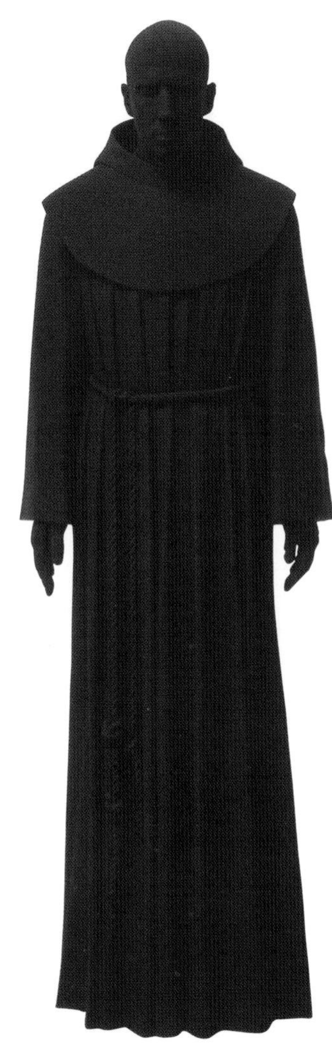

Katharina Fritsch, MÖNCH, 1999
Polyester and paint, 76 x 23 x 17 inches
Courtesy Matthew Marks Gallery, New York

image of Snow White no longer gives us a visage that is white as the driven snow suggests the promise of stories that are attuned to the realities of multicultural communities of readers. We can still engage the old stories and interrogate them for what they tell us about the past, but we produce new images and stories that resonate with our own aesthetic and ethical values.

A few weeks ago, a colleague wrote to me about his plan to write a childhood memoir about encounters with stories such as "Snow White" and "Cinderella." The stories, he reported, played a key role in his "outlook on the world." "One of my earliest memories," he added, "was the sad realization that I could not truly identify with the heroes and heroines of these stories because I was Asian—a fact reinforced by the reminder that I was of Japanese ancestry and came from a race that was an enemy of the United States."

The real wisdom of the old wives' tales from the past is encapsulated in the reminder that these tales, as much as they may reflect the local and the particular, have a global reach. The Chinese girl with a small foot who attends a festival in a cloak of kingfisher feathers has a good deal in common with the French girl who loses her glass slipper on the steps of a castle. The disobedient German girl wearing a red cap as she wanders through the woods is a close cousin of the Italian trickster on her way to grandmother's house. As Marina Warner tells us, "The hearthside crone who passes on the wisdom of the tribe, who epitomizes the once upon a time when all was well, has always been a polyglot cosmopolitan, in spite of her homely headshawl and those old, regional clogs she wears and her funny beaked nose and her spinning wheel" (Warner 1995, 111). In weaving stories and creating images inspired by what that polyglot cosmopolitan whispered in our ears when we were young, we revitalize our cultural heritage, reclaiming its plots but also transforming them into our own.

Karen Arm, UNTITLED (STARS), 2000
Acrylic on canvas, 44 x 36 inches
Courtesy of PPOW, New York

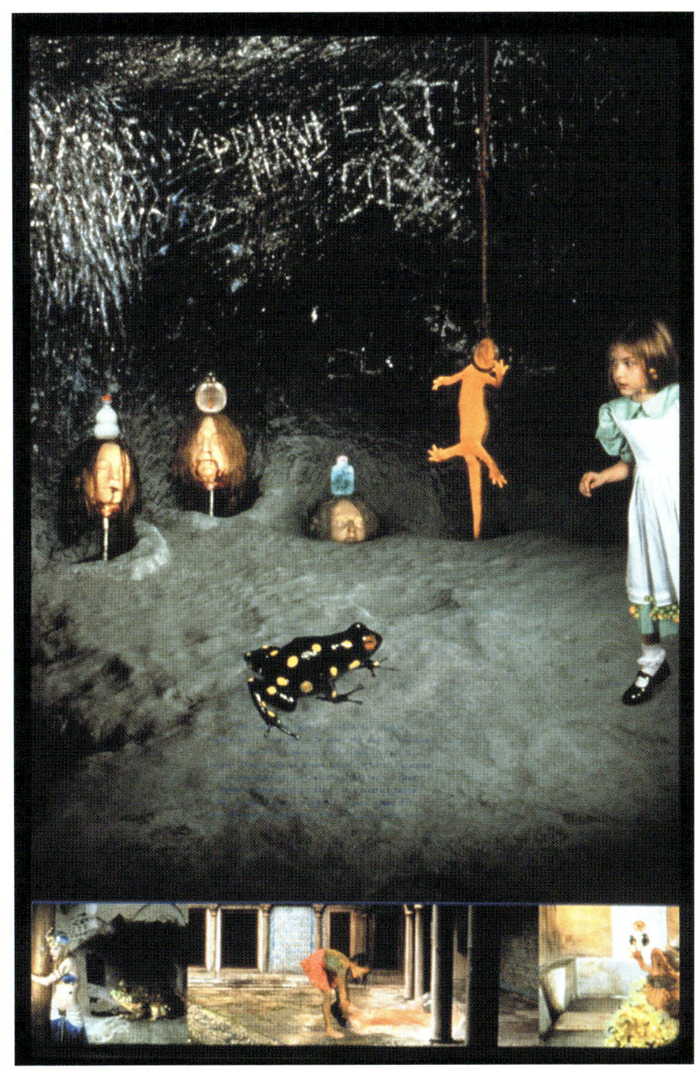

Meghan Boody, PSYCHE SEES, 2000
Fujiflex print, 56 1/2 x 41 1/2 inches
Courtesy Sandra Gering Gallery, New York

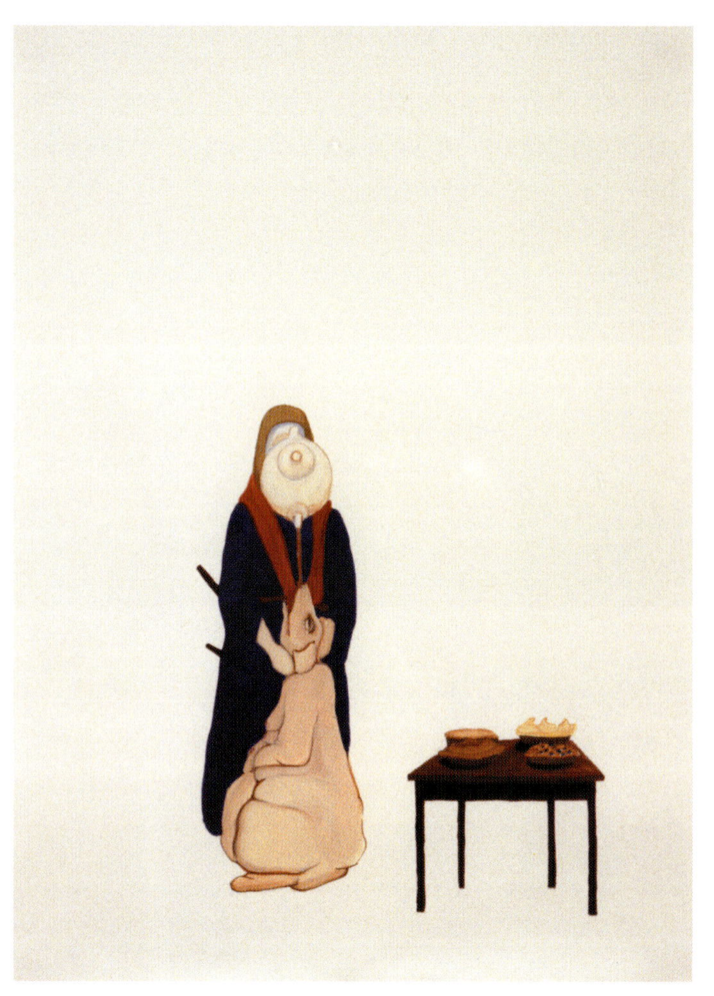

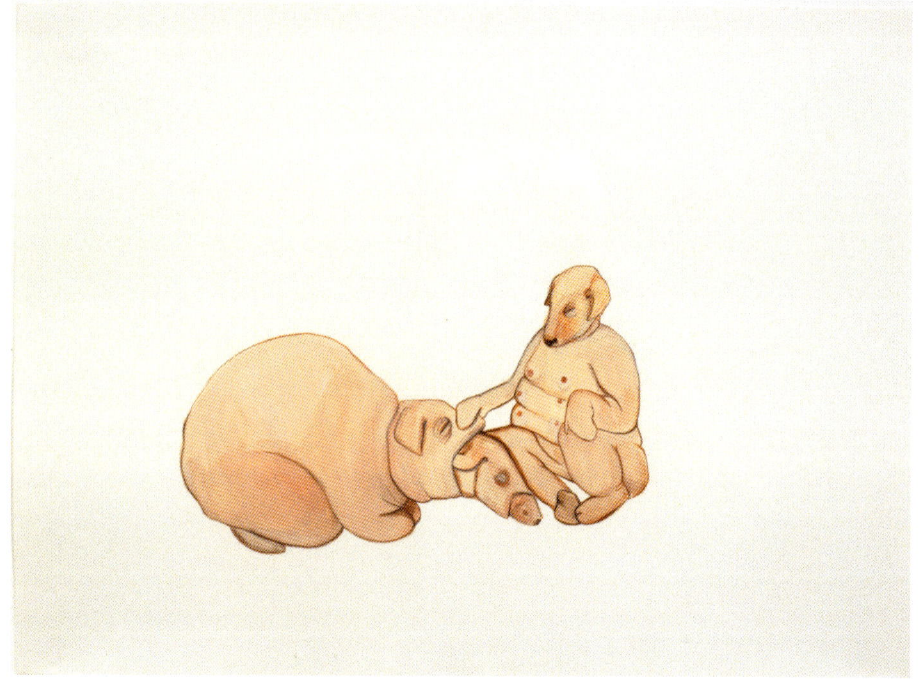

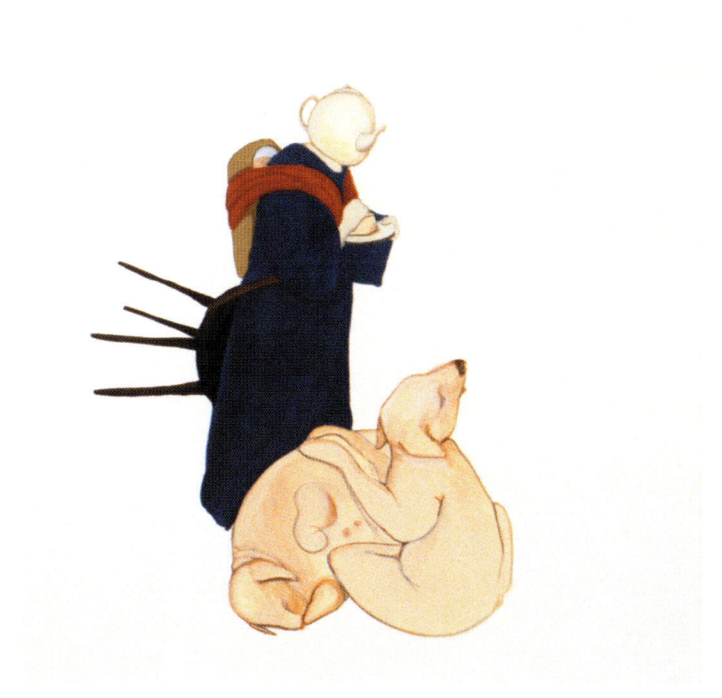

Amy Cutler,TEA POT HEAD, 1997
Gouache on paper, 17 x 13 inches
13 x 17 inches, 17 x 13 inches
Courtesy the artist

An ugly duckling becomes a beautiful swan. The overlooked and mistreated servant becomes the most beautiful and desirable woman at the royal ball. A frog becomes a handsome prince. So it goes in fairy tales, an unstable realm where objects are magical and personalities are in constant flux. Creatures and people are not always what they seem. The helpless old lady is actually a powerful fairy, or the hapless third son turns out to be the most successful member of the household. At the heart of many fairy tales is transformation and change.

As a literary genre, fairy tales are rather fluid in that they are considered children's texts as well as adult texts. Folk and fairy tales are much more complicated and subtle than many people think—they certainly have never been nor will ever be just simple stories created to educate and entertain children. They never have been and never will be. As British folklorists Iona and Peter Opie suggest in their "Introduction" to *Classic Fairy Tales*, "Further analysis may show the tale to be even less like the popular conception of them" (12). Rather than being simple stories for simple minds, the Opies argue that "Perhaps after all, fairy tales are to be numbered the most philosophic tales that there are." (12).

While fairy tales have become an important aspect of children's literature, they didn't start out that way. Folk tales were simply tales of the folk. As part of the oral tradition, the primary audience for folk tales was adult, although undoubtedly some children were listening.

When scholars Jacob and Wilhem Grimm were collecting folk tales for their collection *Kinder—und Hausmärchen* [1812, 1814], they initially thought they were preserving German culture for future scholars and did not consider children as their readers. For the Grimms, fairy tales were *like* children, not *for* children.

The same is true for literary fairy tales, those stories with specific authors who use folk tales as their models. While the best known of the French literary fairy tales are those written by Charles Perrault and published as *Histories ou contes du temps passé: Contes de Ma Mere L'Oye* [1697], it was Marie-Catherine d'Aulnoy and other women writers who helped develop the popularity of fairy tales among the French aristocracy during the late seventeenth century. It is from the title of d'Aulnoy's collection *Les Contes des fées* [1678, 1679], which was translated into English as *Tales of the Fairies,* from that the term "fairy tale" is derived.

J.R.R. Tolkien has suggested in his essay "On Fairy-stories" that, "the association of children and fairy stories is an accident of our domestic history. Fairy stories have in the modern lettered word been relegated to the 'nursery,' as shabby or old-fashioned furniture is relegated to the playroom, primarily because the adults do not want it, and do not mind if it is misused" (34).

While I have always appreciated Tolkien's metaphor of the fairy tale as a piece of furniture, the journey of fairy tale from adult literature to children's literature is a bit

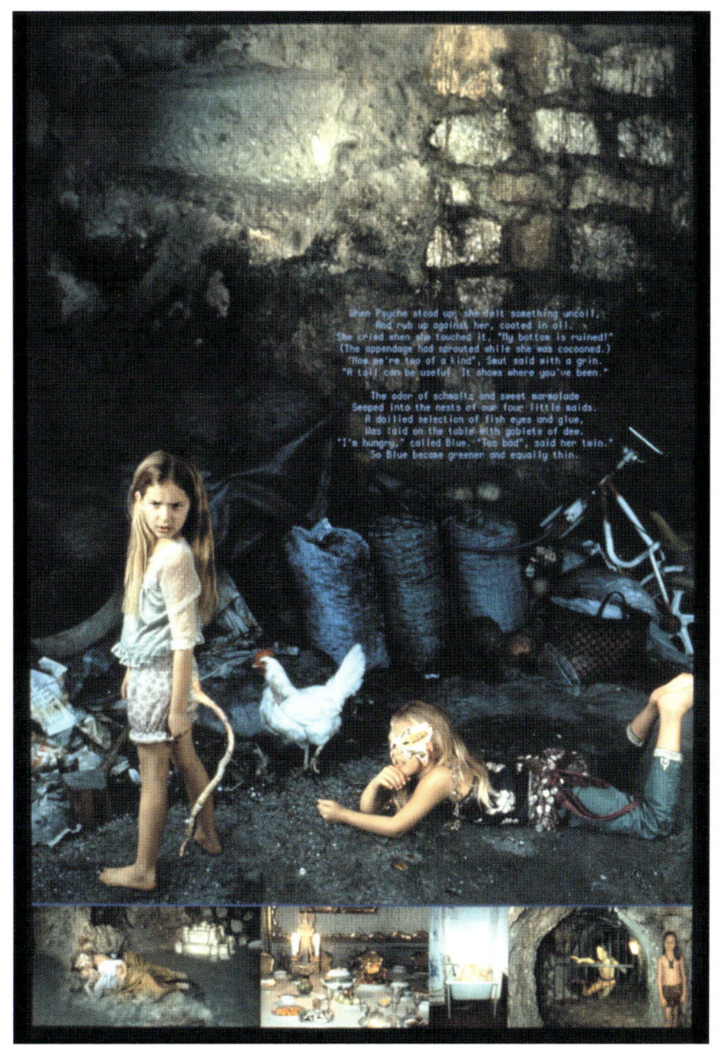

Meghan Boody, PSYCHE'S TAIL, 2000
Fujiflex print, 56 1/2 x 41 1/2 inches
Courtesy Sandra Gering Gallery, New York

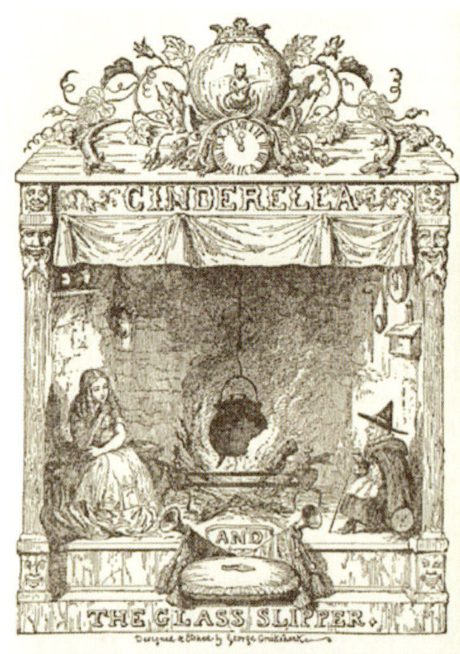

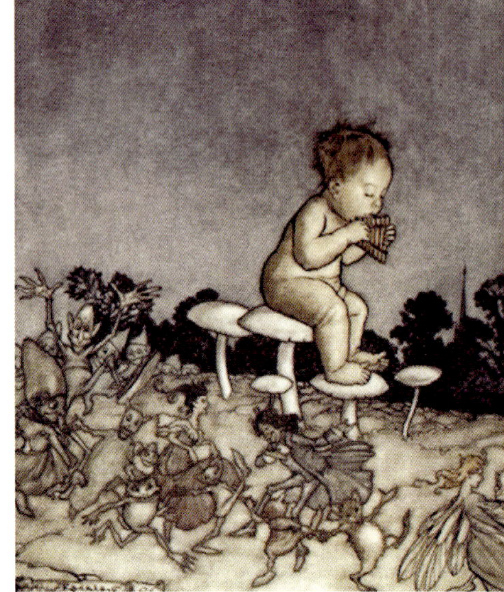

George Cruikshank. Cinderella illustration from *German Popular Stories*, 1823, 1826.

Arthur Rackham, illustration from *Peter Pan in Kensington Gardens*, 1906.

more convoluted and ought to go on a little further. If it is a well made piece of furniture and survives for a hundred years or more, finally someone is going to go down to the basement, realize it is an antique, and put it back into the front parlor where it once again becomes an object of adult admiration.

Fairy tales have been around for hundreds, if not thousands, of years. They are powerful stories with amazing characters and plots that can be endlessly expanded and revised. Take "Beauty and the Beast," add Charlotte Brontë, and you get *Jane Eyre.* You get the idea: fairy tales started out as adult tales, lost their status and became children's literature, but now have been reclaimed by adult readers.

When Edgar Taylor translated Grimm's tales into English as *German Popular Stories* [1823, 1826] he wrote in his "Preface" that he intended the stories "to tickle the palate of the young" (iii), and in order to direct the fairy tales toward child readers, he had the collection illustrated by the popular graphic artist George Cruikshank. Cruikshanks's brilliant black-and-white etchings are regarded as the high point of British book illustration, as Gordon Ray has noted in *The Illustrator and the Book in England.* John Ruskin considered Cruikshank's illustrations to *German Popular Stories* equal to etchings by Rembrandt. With their comic sensibility and grotesque use of detail, Cruikshank's images were pivotal in making fairy tales and literary fairy tales two of the most popular forms of children's literature during the Victorian period. Indeed, the nineteenth century was a golden age of children's literature in general, and of fairy tales in particular. The period began with the publication of *Grimm's Fairy Tales* in English and ended with Andrew Lang's famous twelve-volume collection of fairy tales from around the world, illustrated by H.J. Ford. Lang's first volume, *The Blue Fairy Book*, was published in 1889. In addition to volumes of traditional tales, the nineteenth century also saw the publication of outstanding literary fairy tales by writers such as Hans Christian Anderson, Lewis Carroll, Christina Rossetti, George MacDonald, and J.M. Barrie.

The popularity of fairy tales during the Victorian period was not limited to literary versions. Fairy tales became the basis for the pantomime, a popular theatrical form which appealed both to children and adults. James Barrie's *Peter Pan*, the well known children's play, is now part of that pantomime tradition, best exemplifying how fairy tales slip between child and adult audiences. *Peter Pan* was first introduced as an interpolated story in Barrie's adult novel *Little White Bird* [1902]. Barrie would produce the first theatrical production of *Peter Pan*, *or The Boy Who Wouldn't Grow Up* in 1904, followed by *Peter Pan in Kensington Gardens* [1906], an expensive illustrated edition by Arthur Rackham intended for adults. The children's novel *Peter and Wendy* was published in 1911. Barrie's final publication of the story was the script of *Peter Pan* in 1928, by which time the original three-act play had grown into a five-act play. These mul-

tiple versions by Barrie do not account for subsequent film revisions ranging from Walt Disney's *Peter Pan* [1953] to Steven Spielberg's *Hook* [1991].

Stephen Sondheim and James Lapine's popular Broadway musical *Into the Woods* [1987] helped reintroduce fairy tales as adult entertainment. *Into the Woods* was strongly influenced by the playwright's reading of Bruno Bettelheim's *The Uses of Enchantment: The Meaning and Importance of Fairy Tales*, which was a psychological interpretation of how children use fairy tales to cope with events of their in their lives—once again demonstrating the shift from children's to adult texts and vice versa.

Most significantly for the artwork that appears in *pixerina*WITCHERINA, England also experienced from 1840 to 1875 a flurry of fairy paintings influenced in part by the popularity of fairy tales and literary fairy tales. Famous children's picture book illustrators—such as Walter Crane, Randolph Caldecott, and Kate Greenaway—all drew their fair share of fairies, but so did artists whose work was primarily viewed by adults such as Dante Gabriel Rossetti, J.M.W Turner, and John Everett Millais. The recent exhibition *Victorian Fairy Painting,* organized by the University of Iowa Museum of Art and the Royal Academy of Arts, London, as well as Christopher Wood's *Fairies in Victorian Art*, have revived interest in this once popular art form. While well-established artists occasionally drew a fairy painting, the genre was dominated by a

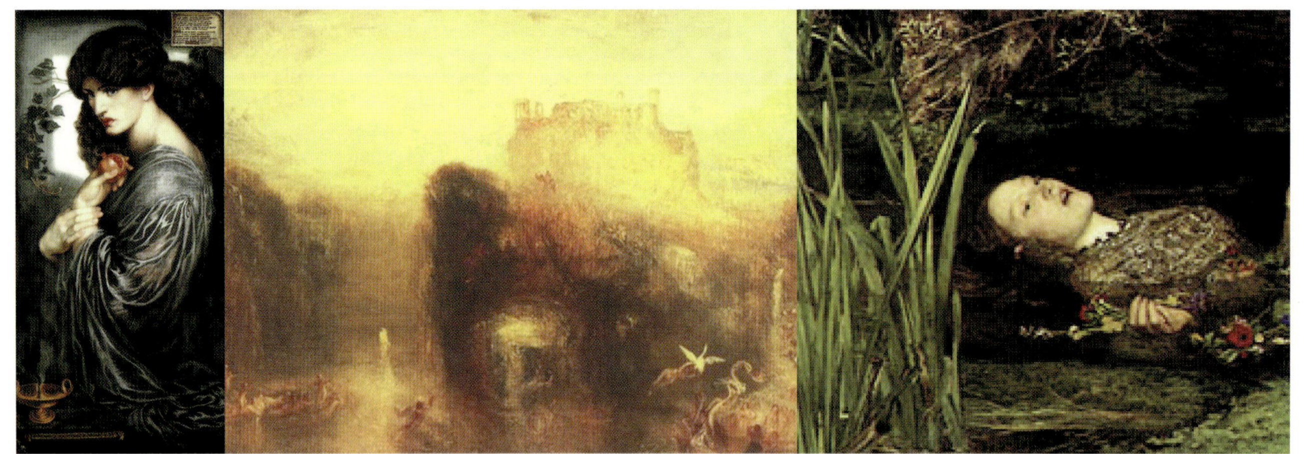

Dante Gabriel Rossetti, *Prosperine (Persephone)*, 1874.

J.M.W. Turner, *Queen Mab's Cave*, 1846.

John Everett Millais, *Ophelia* detail, 1851-2.

handful of artists who specialized in fairies including John Anster Fitzerald, nicknamed "Fairy Fitzgerald," Robert Huskisson, and Richard Doyle. The most famous fairy painter is the unfortunate Richard Dadd, who is considered by Jeremy Maas in his essay "Victorian Fairy Painting" to be the "quintessential fairy painter" (14). While Dadd exhibited several fairy paintings at the Royal Academy in the 1840s, he produced what are considered to be his masterpieces, *Contradiction: Oberon and Titania* [1854-58] and *The Fairy Feller's Master Stroke* [1855-64], after his confinement to the Bethlem Royal Hospital for murdering his father. Maas has suggested that fairy painting, more than most other genres, was intimately linked to the exploration of the subconscious, an observation that also applies to the work in *pixerina*WITCHERINA. In his essay "Fairies and the Stage," Lionel Lambourne has warned that "the politics of fairyland are never correct"

(47): Victorian fairy painting allowed artists to explore conflicting attitudes toward sexuality, as well as to touch on the unknown and forbidden. While Maureen Duffy's *The Erotic World of Faery* examines in detail the strong erotic impulse in fairy art and fairy tales, Carol Silver's *Strange and Secret Peoples: Fairies and Victorian Consciousness* sees in Victorian fairy painting as a strong tendency toward violence and cruelty. Other critics have suggested that fairy painting was simply a ploy to paint and exhibit nudes by adding wings to human figures. The majority of fairy painters were males, although there are number of notable exceptions, including the still popular and overly sentimental Cecily Mary Barker's flower fairies and Estella Canziani's extremely popular image "The Piper of Dreams," which became a great favorite of World War I soldiers.

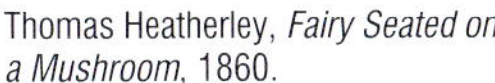

John Simmons, *Titania*, 1866.

Joseph Noel Paton, *The Quarrel of Oberon and Titania*, 1849.

Thomas Heatherley, *Fairy Seated on a Mushroom*, 1860.

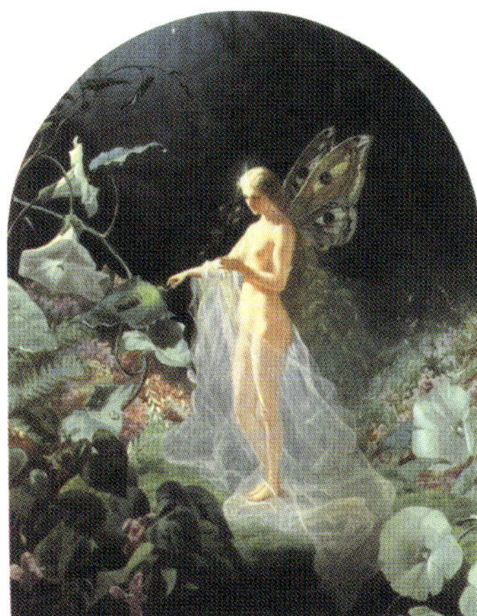

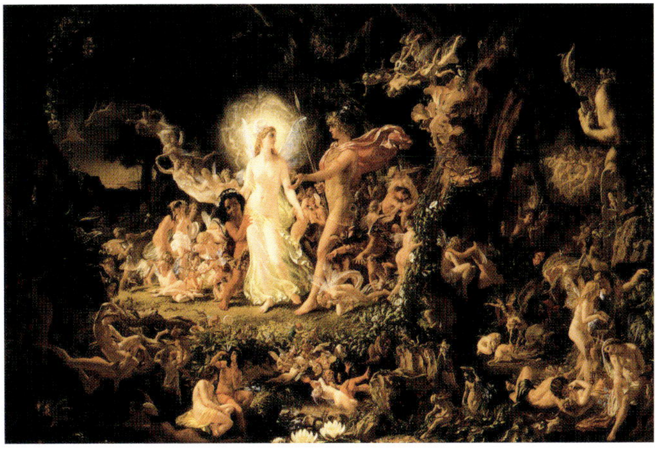

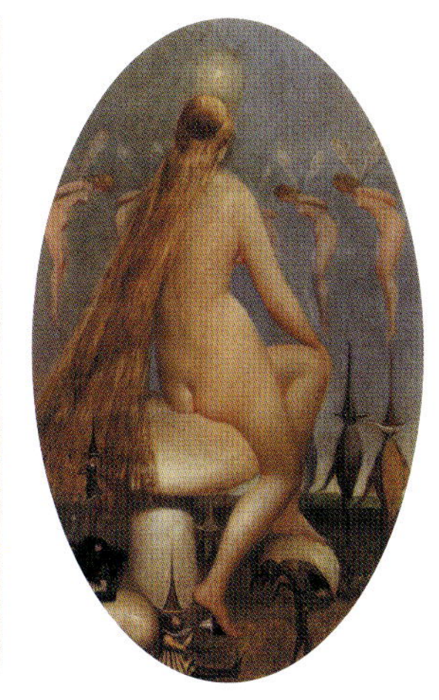

What is striking about the images in *pixerina*WITCHERINA is how little they have in common with Victorian fairy painting. Clearly gender has much to do with this. Rejecting the sexy female nude that was commonplace in Victorian fairy painting, these artists are consciously trying to reclaim fairy tales as a female tradition visually re-imagined from a female point of view. Rather than eroticized young fairies, Margi Geerlinks' TWINS is a photograph of two elderly women confronting each other and the mirror on the wall. Like other art in this exhibit, TWINS seems to be strongly influenced by the ongoing feminist revisiond of fairy tales. For example, Anne Sexton's *Transformations* is a stunning reinterpretation of *Grimm's Fairy Tales* into something very modern, something very adult, which is in is keeping with confessional poetry for which Sexton was best known. Angela Carter's *The Bloody Chamber* is a strong prose revision of Charles Perrault's fairy tales taken from the female protagonists' point of view. Both Wolfgang Mieder's *Disenchantments: An Anthology of Modern Fairy Tales Poetry* and Jack Zipes's *Don't Bet on the Prince: Contemporary Feminist Fairy Tales in North America and England* are varied collections of recent revisions of fairy tales for adults.

Revisionist fairy tales are also common in recent children's and adolescent literature. John Scieszka and Lane Smith's *The Stinky Cheeseman and Other Fairy Stupid Tales* is visually and verbally a brilliant postmodern picture book adaptation of a series of fairy tales. Their earlier collaboration, *The True Story of the Three Little Pigs Told By A. Wolf*, finds the wolf declaring his innocence and blaming his situation on the media. David Wiesner's *The Three Pigs*, like *The Stinky Cheeseman*, decon-

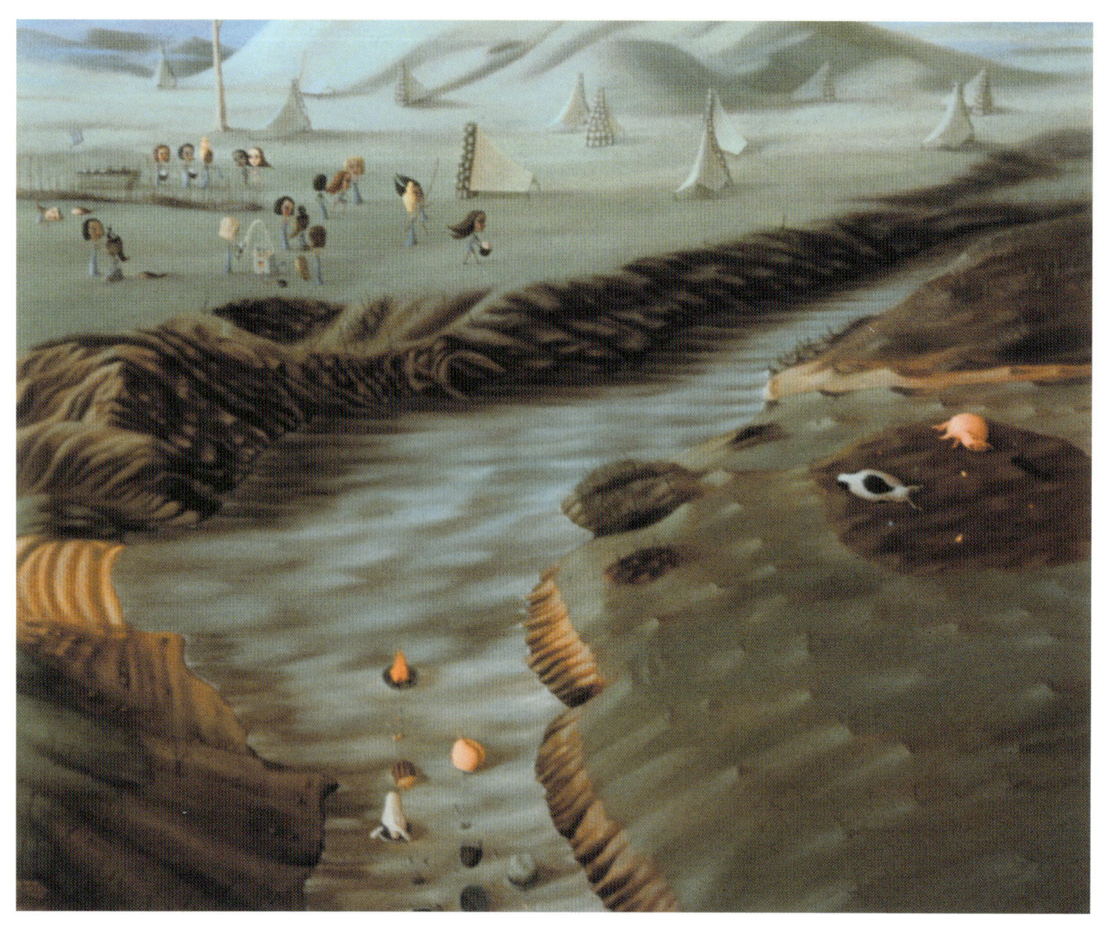

Hilary Harkness, DYING FROM HOME AND LOST, 1998
Oil on panel, 23 1/2 x 29 inches
Courtesy Bill Maynes Gallery, New York

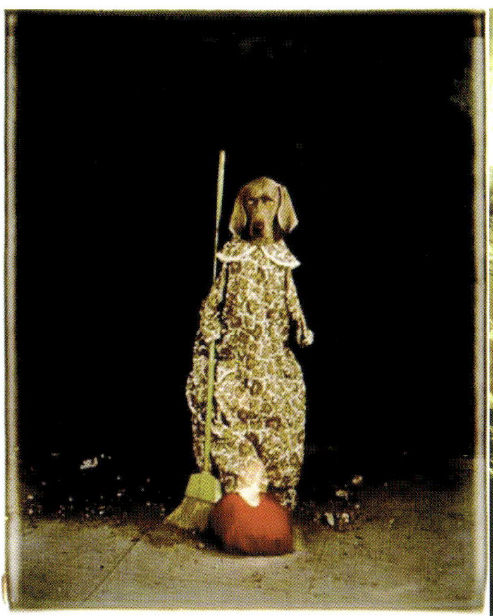

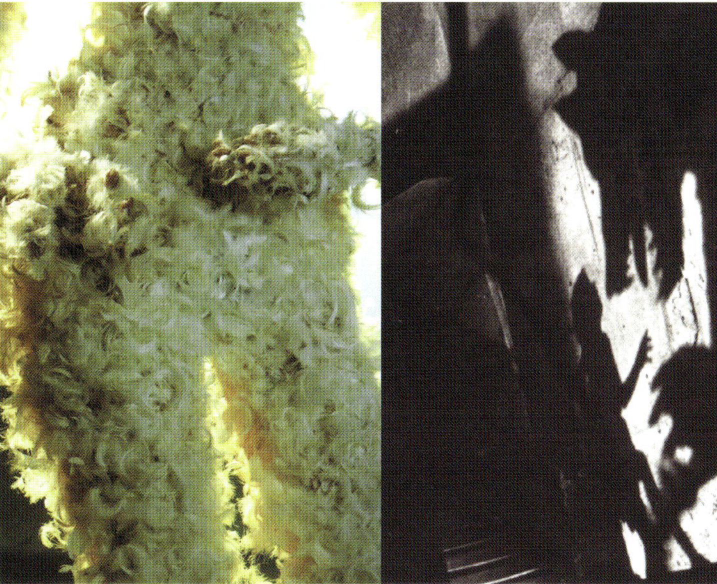

William Wegman, *Cinderella With Glass Slipper*, 1993.

Cindy Sherman, illustrative photograph from *Fitcher's Bird*, 1992.

Sarah Moon, illustrative photograph from *Little Red Riding Hood* 1983. Text by Charles Perrault.

structs the concept of a children's picture book. When Art Speigelman and Françoise Mouly edit *Little Lit: Folklore & Fairy Tale Funnies*—a collection of illustrated fairy tales which combine well-known children's picture book illustrators such as David Macaulay and William Joyce with adult comic book artists such as Chris Ware and Kaz—you know that the boundaries between adult and children's texts are extremely fluid. William Wegman's "Fay's Fairy Tales" series, including *Little Red Riding Hood* and *Cinderella,* feature color photographs of his Weimaraner oddly costumed as the fairy tale characters. Cindy Sherman's photographs of posed mannequins in *Fitcher's Bird* is another disturbing illustration of one of Grimm's fairy tales. Sarah Moon's chilling black-and-white photographs update Perrault's *Little Red Riding Hood*: a young girl is hunted down city streets by a limousine's headlights. These seem similar in tone to two photographs by Meghan Boody, PSYCHE SEES and PSYCHE'S TAIL, which are part of a longer photographic sequence involving a contemporary Alice and her looking-glass double's adventures beneath the streets of New York City.

Lewis Carroll and his literary fairy tale *Alice's Adventures in Wonderland* [1865] seems referenced in several of the works in the exhibit, including Katharina Fritsch's sound installation MUHLE, KRANKENWAGEN, UNKEN (MILL, AMBULANCE, TOADS). Here the artist combines found sounds with remembered symbols of her childhood, echoing the conclusion of Carroll's *Alice's Adventures in*

Wonderland when Alice awakes from her dream and tells it to her older sister. Alice's sister in turn falls into her own dream of Wonderland, but realizes that she has transformed the ordinary sounds she hears around her into the magic and mystery of Alice's Wonderland. Julia Latané's FAIRY RING, with its tall series of mushrooms, transforms the viewer into a tiny, but curious Alice struggling to peer over the tops of the gargantuan fungi. Amy Culter's endlessly reproducing rabbits, featured in RABBITS, TEA POT HEAD, and EGG COLLECTION, remind one of Alice's numerous size transformations. But it is Margi Geerlinks' UNTITLED (GIRL) which perhaps has the most surprisingly similarity to Lewis Carroll. In addition to writing Alice's *Adventures in Wonderland* and its sequel *Through the Looking-Glass* [1872], Carroll is known as one of the great photographers of children in the nineteenth century; he specialized in portraits of young girls, including Alice Liddel, for whom he wrote *Alice's Adventures in Wonderland*. The girl in Geerkin's photograph is holding a small silver mushroom, but more significantly the young girl's stance seems to update Carroll's

1857 photograph of Agnes Grace Weld as Little Red Riding Hood (Gernsheim, *Lewis Carroll Photographer*, Plate 10) in that both figures are coming out of the darkened background with same tilted head peering intently into the camera.

Other children's texts are referenced in the exhibition as well, most overtly in Claudia Hart's work. NIGHTMARE FOR TINKY-WINKY refers to the popular children's television program *Teletubbies*, but within the painting Hart has doubled the image of the young girl who foolishly plays with matches in Heinrich Hoffman's darkly ironic poem, which appeared in his self-illustrated picture book *Struwwelpeter* [1845]. The same poem was featured as one of songs in Martyn Jacques's *Shockeheaded Peter: A Junk Opera*, which featured the music by the Tiger Lillies. In A LOVE STORY INVOLVING TWO GUYS, Hart reproduced the Rat who tried to turn the innocent Tom Kitten into a roly-poly pudding for dinner in Beatrix Potter's *The Tale of Samuel Whiskers* [1908]. With these details, Hart reminds the viewer that much of children's literature is not all a "big hug" as

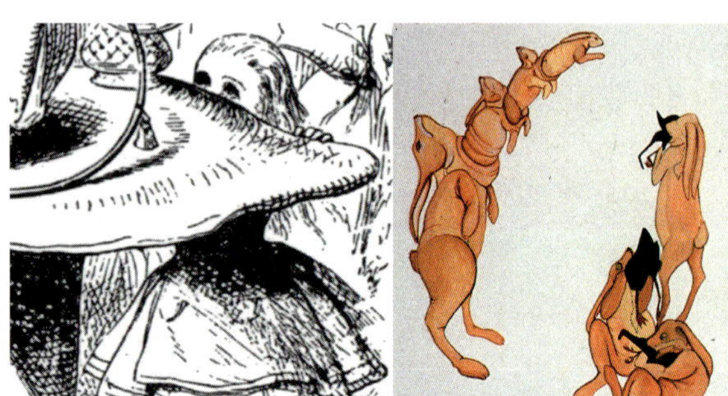

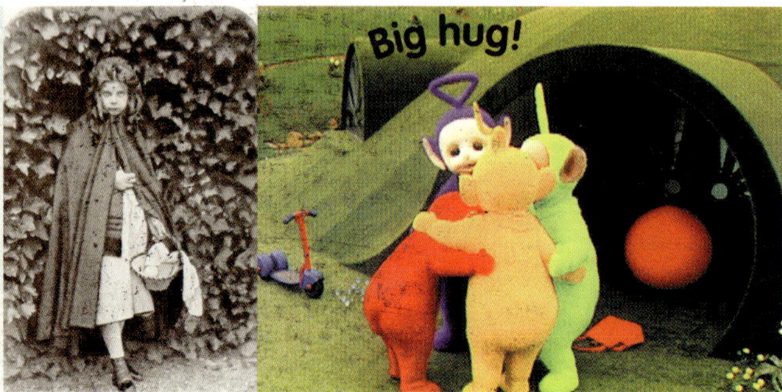

John Tenniel, illustration from *Alice's Adventures in Wonderland*.

Amy Cutler, RABBITS detail, 1996. Courtesy Eyewash, New York.

Lewis Carroll, Agnes Grace Weld as Little Red Riding Hood, 1857.

Teletubbies "big hug."

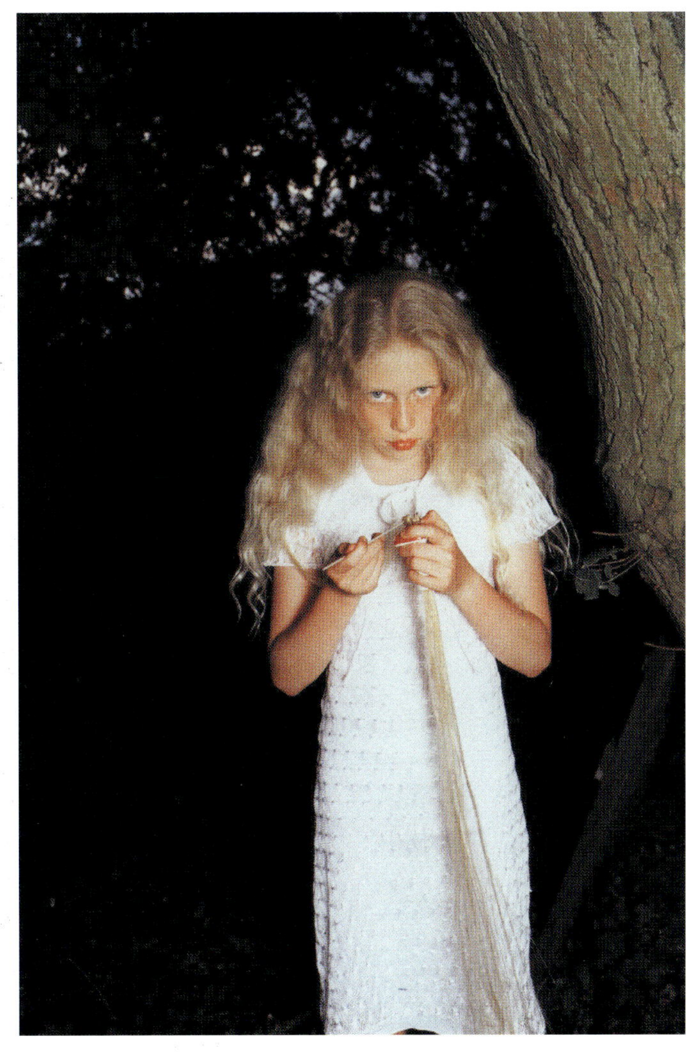

Margi Geerlinks, UNITITLED (GIRL), 1999
Fujichrome, perspex, and dibond, 60 x 49 1/4 inches
Courtesy Stefan Stux, New York
Photo: Karl Rademacher

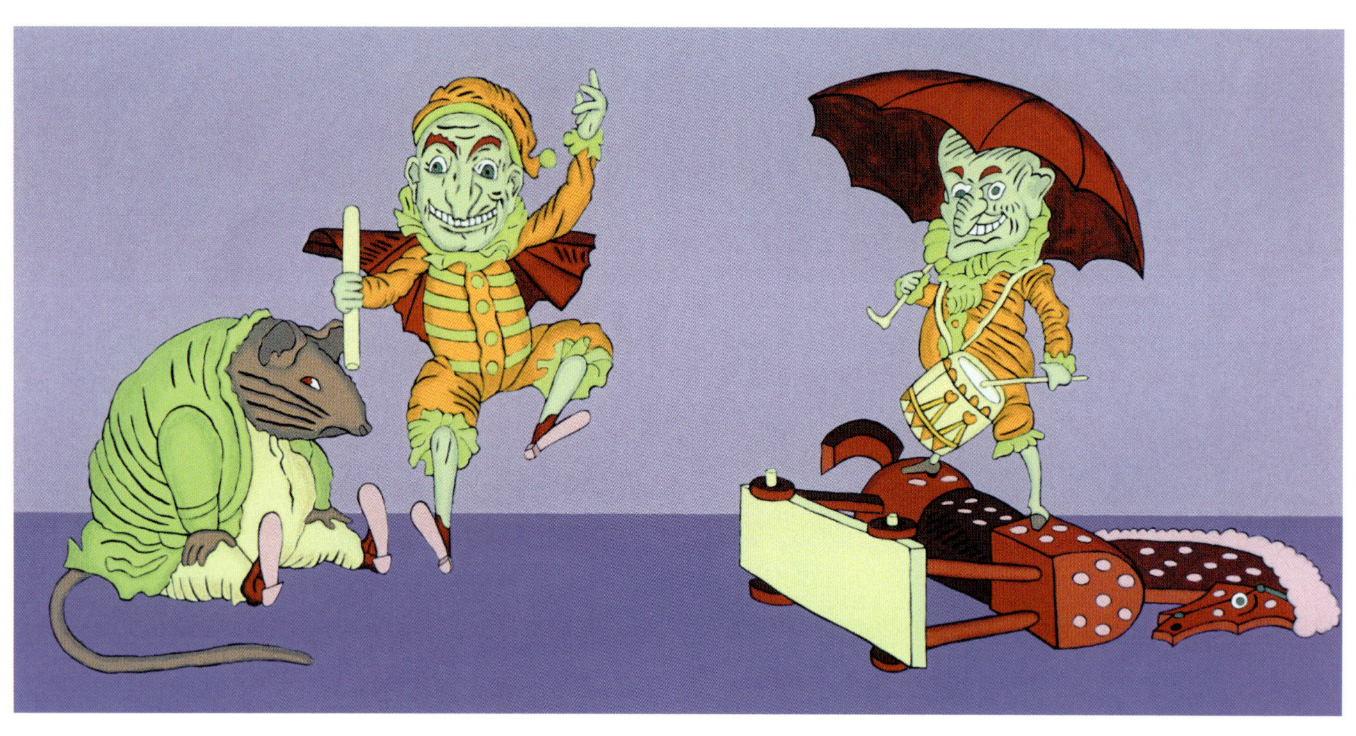

Claudia Hart, A NIGHTMARE FOR TINKY WINKY, 1998
Acrylic on canvas, 30 x 60 inches
Courtesy Sandra Gering Gallery, New York

on *Teletubbies*, but is actually full of darkness and dread. It is fitting that the curator for this exhibit, Bill Conger, has chosen to name it *pixerina*WITCHERINA, in that the title refers to an imaginary language created by Virginia Woolf to secretly converse with her niece. As a feminist writer and critic, Woolf argued in her essay "Professions for Women" that, "Killing the Angel in the house was part of the occupation of a woman writer" (279). In other words, women need to rid themselves of male-generated stereotypes which cast them as either good or evil. The artists in this exhibition have taken Woolf's dictum to heart and killed off the predominately male tradition of Victorian fairy painting. Literary references to   William Shakespeare inspired most Victorian fairy paintings. So it seems appropriate that Virginia Woolf, in *A Room of One's Own* [1929], would propose the creation of an alternative female literary tradition based on "Shakespeare's sister," a tradition of creativity which has been either lost or ignored in a male-dominated world. Following Woolf's lead, the artists in *pixerina*WITCHERINA create their own distinctively female visual interpretations of fairy tales. Taken as a group, they have much more in common with the alternative female literary tradition proposed by Virginia Woolf in *A Room of One's Own* and in the revisionist fairy tales of Angela Carter and Anne Sexton than with earlier fairy art. Younger writers— such as Francesca Lia Block in books such as *I Was a Teenage Fairy* and *The Rose and the Beast: Fairy Tales Retold*, or Emma Donoghue in *Kissing the Witch: Old Tales in New Skins*—are continu-

ing this tradition of rewriting fairy tales intended for adolescents, with distinctive gender-bending approaches and eroticism from a female perspective. In killing off the angel of the house, what remains is the fairy. Suza Scalora, whose haunting photographs of fairies have appeared on the covers of several of Block's adolescent novels, has recently published a collection of artwork titled *The Fairies: Photographic Evidence of the Existence of Another World*. These are powerful and self-willed creatures who don't appear to spend much time around the house.But as L. Frank Baum, the author of the great American fairy tale, *The Wonderful Wizard of Oz*, wrote in his essay "Modern Fairy Tales," "A fairy has wings, and is much like an angel, only smaller" (137). Maybe these contemporary fairies are smaller, but they are distinctly feminist. Modern fairy tales and fairy images are no longer created by male artists as a way to gaze at women, but created by women for women in an attempt to reclaim a lost tradition. Once again, the fairy tale has transformed itself.

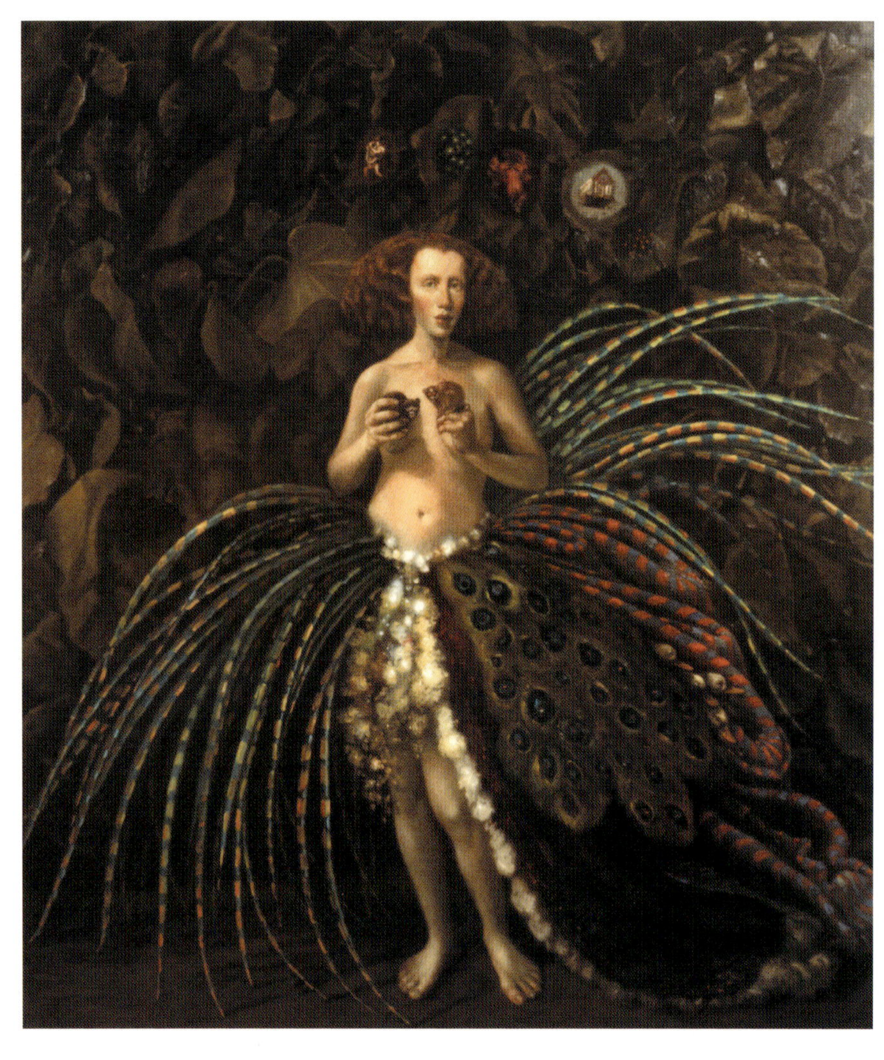

Julie Heffernan,
SELF-PORTRAIT AS INFANTA DREAMING MADAME DE SADE, 1999
Oil on canvas, 67 x 58 inches
Courtesy P·P·O·W, New York

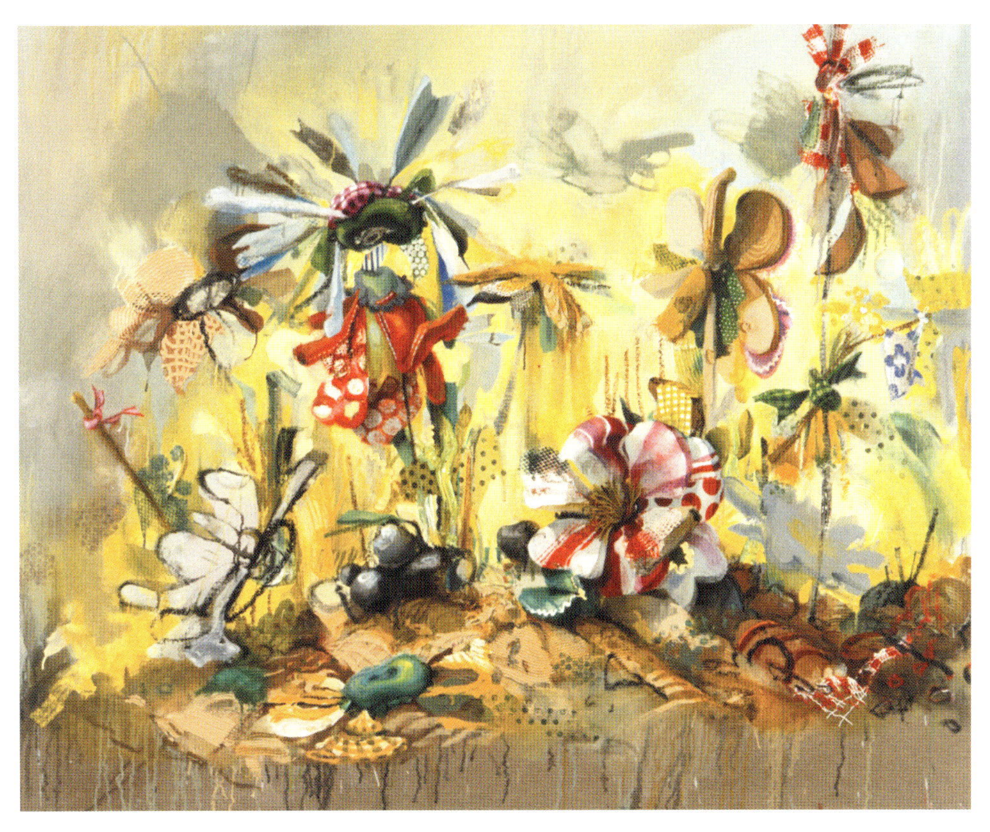

Margaret Curtis, THE LANGUAUGE OF FLOWERS, 1999
Oil on linen, 48 x 60 inches
Courtesy P·P·O·W, New York

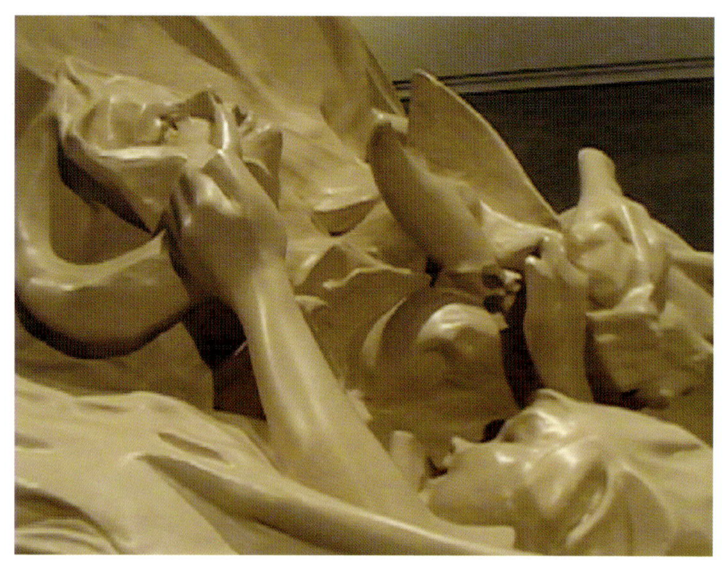

above: **Bonnie Collura**, THE PURSUIT OF HAPPINESS (detail)
Photo: Karl Rademacher

below: Giovanni Lorenzo Bernini, *The Blessed Ludovica Albertoni* (detail), San Francesco a Ripa, 1674

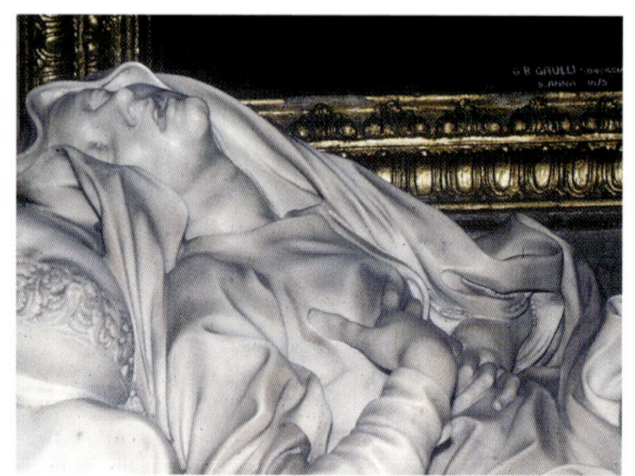

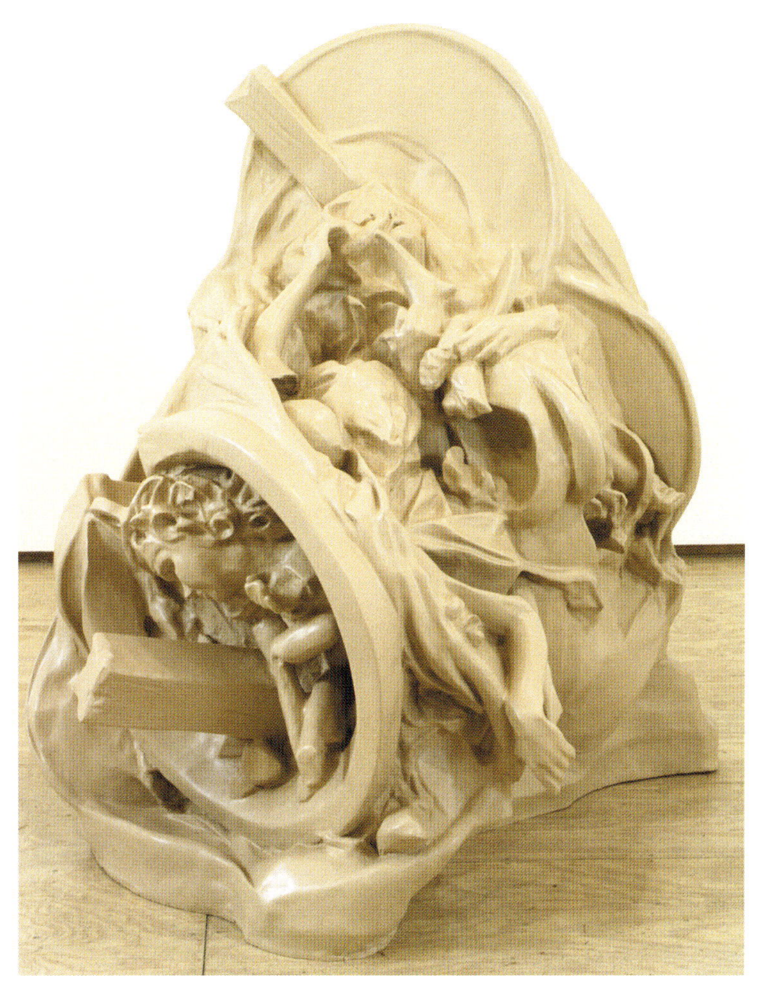

Bonnie Collura, THE PURSUIT OF HAPPINESS, 1999
Fiberglass, resin and paint, 67 x 53 x 44 inches
Courtesy Lehmann Maupin Gallery, New York

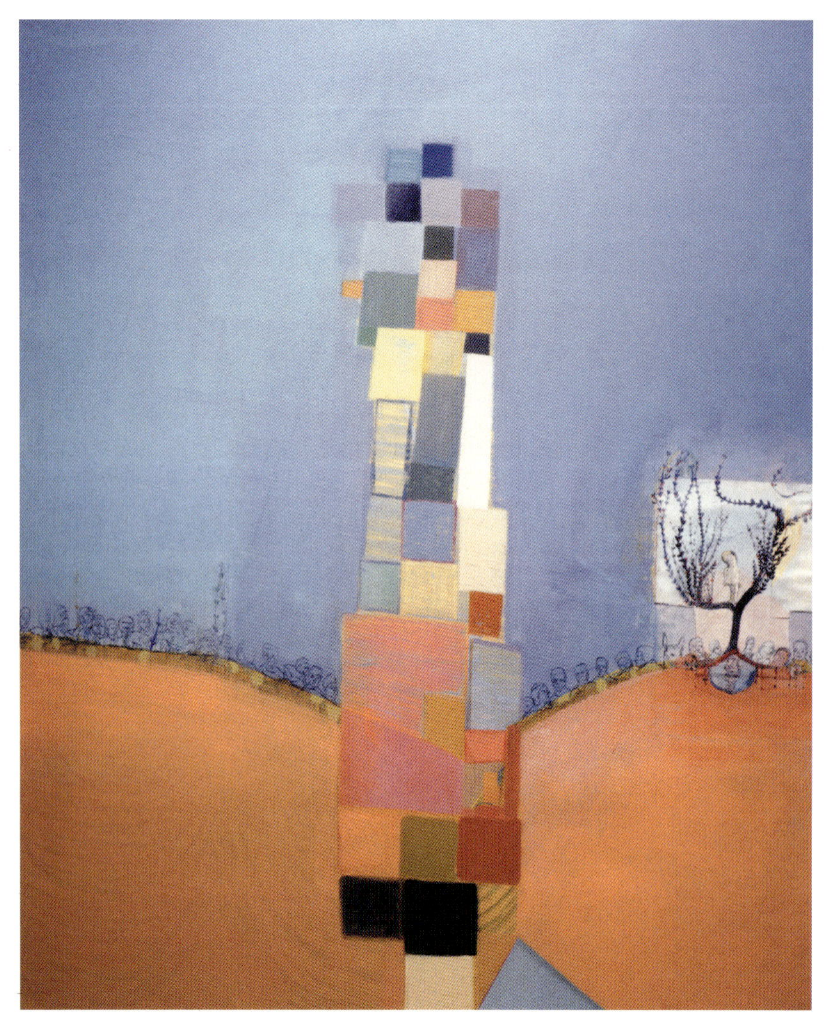

Amy Sillman, FREUDIAN SLIP, 2000
Oil on canvas, 60 x 50 inches
Collection Gregory Miller, New York

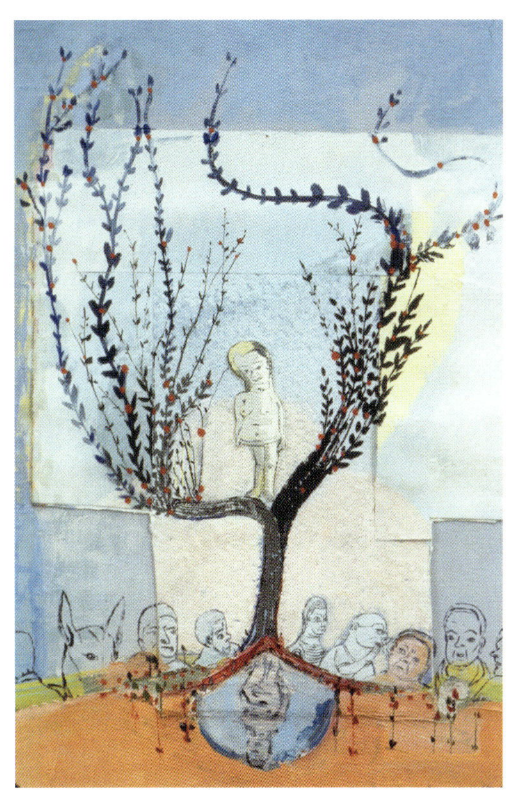

Amy Sillman, FREUDIAN SLIP (detail)

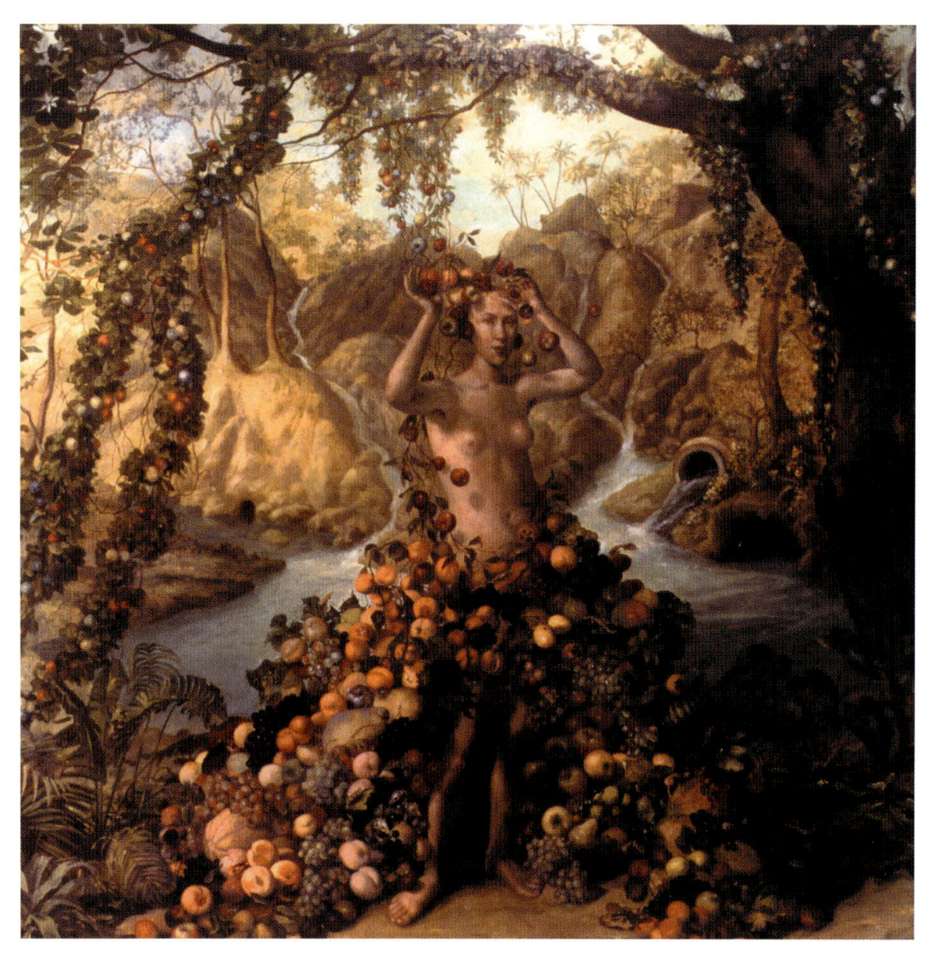

Julie Heffernan, SELF-PORTRAIT AS RADIANT HOST, 2000
Oil on canvas, 83 x 84 inches
Courtesy of P·P·O·W, New York

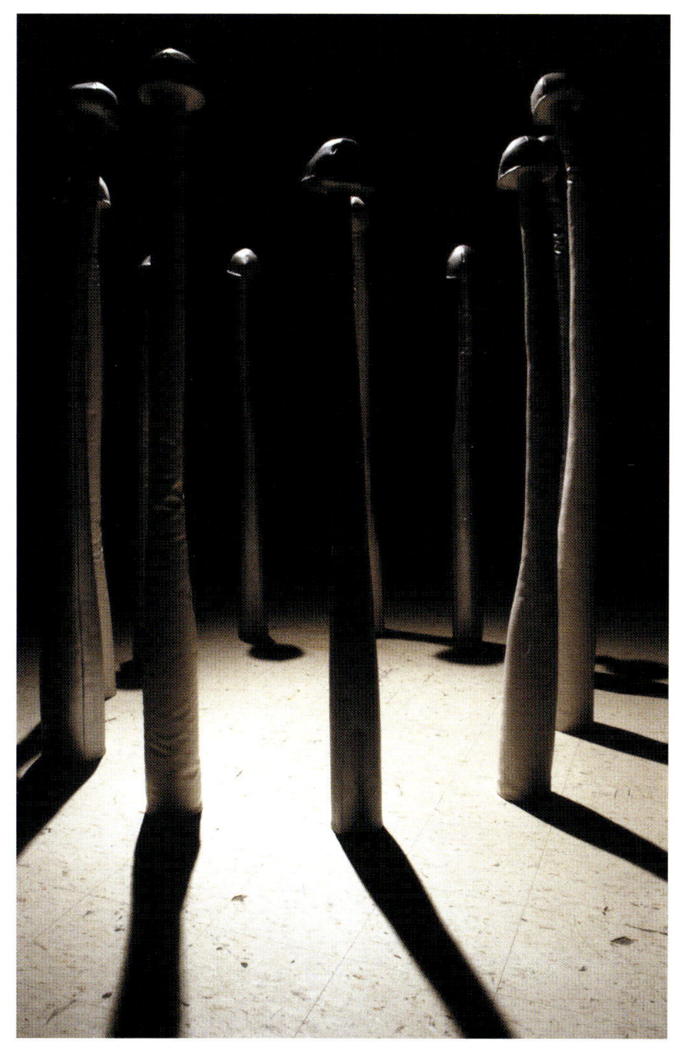

Julia Latané, FAIRY RING, 1999
Vinyl, 10 x 10 x 7 feet
Courtesy the artist
Photo: Karl Rademacher

NOTES AND BIBLIOGRAPHY

WHAT BIG TEETH by Bill Conger.

1. Hermione Lee. *Virginia Woolf: A Working Life*. London, 1996. pp. 547-8.
2. Marina Warner. *No Go The Bogeyman*. New York: Farrar, Straus and Giroux, 1998. pp. 262-3.
3. Montague Summers, translator. *Malleus Maleficarum*. London, 1928.
4. I am paraphrasing the Little Red Riding Hood evolution concept from a lecture delivered by Roberta Trites entitled "Stories Women Tell Children" held April 17th, 2001 at University Galleries of Illinois State University.
5. Sigmund Freud. "A seventeenth-century demonological neurosis." *The Ego and the Id and Other Works*. 1923-5. Courtesy the New York Freudian Society: www.nyfreudian.org.

INVOCATIONS OF FAIRY TALES by Maria Tatar.

Atwood, Margaret. "Significant Moments in the Life of My Mother," *Bluebeard's Egg and Other Stories*. New York: Ballantine, Fawcett Crest, 1983. pp. 1-23.
Benjamin, Walter. "The Storyteller: Reflections on the Works of Nikolai Leskov," *Illuminations*. Trans. Harry Zohn. New York: Schocken, 1968. pp. 83-109.
Updike, John. "Fiabe Italiane." In *Hugging the Shore: Essays and Criticism*. New York: Knopf, 1983. pp. 662-65.
Warner, Marina. *From the Beast to the Blonde: On Fairy Tales and Their Tellers*. New York: Farrar, Straus and Giroux, 1994.
___________. *Six Myths of Our Time: Little Angels, Little Monsters, Beautiful Beasts, and More*. New York: Random House, 1995.
Zipes, Jack, Ed. *Beauties, Beasts and Enchantment: Classic French Fairy Tales*. New York: New American Library, 1989.

STRAW INTO GOLD by Jan Susina.

Baum, L. Frank. "Modern Fairy Tales." *The Critical Heritage Series: The Wizard of Oz*. Ed. Michael Patrick Hearn. New York: Schocken Books, 1983. 137-40.
Bettelheim, Bruno. *The Uses of Enchantment: The Meaning and Importance of Fairy Tales*. New York: Knopf, 1977.
Block, Francesa Lia. *I Was a Teenage Fairy*. New York: HarperCollins, 1998.
______________. *The Rose and the Beast: Fairy Tales Retold*. New York: HarperColllins, 2000.
Carroll, Lewis. *Alice's Adventures in Wonderland and Through the Looking-Glass*. 1865, 1872. Ed. Hugh Haughton. New York: Penguin, 1998.
Carter, Angela. *The Bloody Chamber*. New York: Harper & Row, 1979.
Donghue, Emma. *Kissing the Witch: Old Tales in New Skins*. New York: HarperCollins, 1997.
Duffy, Maureen. *The Erotic World of Faery*. New York: Avon, 1972.
Hoffmann, Heinrich. *Struwwelpeter* in English Translation. 1845. Mineola, NY Dover, 1995.

Gernsheim, Helmut. *Lewis Carroll Photographer.* 1949. New York: Dover, 1969.

Grimm, Wilhelm and Jacob. *Fitcher's Bird.* Illustrated by Cindy Sherman. New York: Rizzoli, 1992.

Jacques, Martyn. *Shockheaded Peter: A Junk Opera.* Music by Tiger Lillies. CD, NVC Arts, 1999.

Lambourne, Lionel. "Fairies and the Stage." *Victorian Fairy Painting.* Ed. Jane Martineau. London: Merrell Hoberton, 1997. 46-53.

Maas, Jeremy. "Victorian Fairy Painting." *Victorian Fairy Painting.* Ed. Jane Martineau. London: Merrell Hoberton, 1997. 10-21.

Mieder, Wolfgang, ed. *Disenchantments: An Anthology of Modern Fairy Tale Poetry.* Hanover, NH: University P of New England, 1985.

"Opie, Iona and Peter." Introduction. *The Classic Fairy Tales.* London: OUP, 1974.11-28.

Perrault, Charles. *Little Red Riding Hood.* Illustrated by Sarah Moon. Mankato, MN: Creative Education, 1983.

Ray, Gordon N. *The Illustrator and the Book in England From 1790 to 1914.* New York: Pierpont Morgan Library, 1976.

Scalora, Suza. *The Fairies: Photographic Evidence of the Existence of Another World.* New York: HarperCollins, 1999.

Scieszka, Jon and Lane Smith. *The Stinky Cheeseman and Other Fairly Stupid Tales.* New York: Viking, 1992.

__________________________. *The True Story of The 3 Little Pigs by A. Wolf.* New York: Viking, 1989.

Sexton, Anne. *Transformations.* Boston: Houghton Mifflin, 1971.

Silver, Carol G. *Strange and Secret Peoples: Fairies and Victorian Consciousness.* New York: OUP, 1999.

Sondheim, Stephen and James Lapine. *Into the Woods.* New York: Theatre Communications Group, 1987.

Taylor, Edgar. Preface. *German Popular Stories. 1823-1826.* Facsimile Edition. London: Scholar Press, 1997. Vol. 1: iii-xii.

Tolkien, J.R.R. "On Fairy-stories." *Tree and Leaf.* London: Unwin Books, 1964. 11-70.

Wegman, William. "Cinderella," *Fay's Fairy Tales.* New York: Lookout Books, 1993.

______________. "Little Red Riding Hood," *Fay's Fairy Tales.* New York: Lookout Books, 1993.

Weiser, David. *The Three Pigs.* New York: Clarion Books, 2001.

Wood, Christopher. *Fairies in Victorian Art.* Woodbridge, UK: Antique Collectors' Club, 2000.

Woolf, Virginia. *A Room of One's Own.* 1929. New York: Harper & Row, 1957.

____________. "Professions for Women." *The Virginia Woolf Reader.* Ed Mitchell A Leaksa. New York: Harcourt Brace, 1984. 276-282.

Zipes, Jack. *Don't Bet on the Prince: Contemporary Feminist Fairy Tales in North America and England.* New York: Methuen, 1986.

Karen Arm

UNTITLED (SMOKE #5)
2000
Acrylic on paper
20 x 17 inches

UNTITLED (STARS)
2000
Acrylic on canvas
44 x 36 inches
Both courtesy P·P·O·W

Meghan Boody

PSYCHE SEES
2000
Fujiflex print
56 1/2 x 41 1/2 inches

PSYCHE'S TAIL
2000
Fujiflex print
56 1/2 x 41 1/2 inches
Both courtesy Sandra Gering Gallery

Bonnie Collura

PURSUIT OF HAPPINESS
1999
Fiberglass, resin, and paint
67 x 53 x 44 inches

BERNINI'S PERSEPHONE (CRONE)
1997
Plaster gauzing, foam
10 1/2 x 18 inches
Both courtesy Lehmann Maupin Gallery

Margaret Curtis

BROKEN HORIZON
1998
Oil on linen
24 x 80 inches
Courtesy P·P·O·W

Amy Cutler

RABBITS
1996
Gouache on paper
17 x 22 1/2 inches
Courtesy Eyewash

TEA POT HEAD
1997
Gouache on paper
17 x 13 inches
13 x 17 inches
17 x 13 inches
Courtesy the artist

EGG COLLECTION
1999
Gouache on paper
16 1/2 x 22 3/4 inches
Courtesy Eyewash

Katharina Fritsch

MÜHLE, KRANKENWAGEN, UNKEN
1990
Sound installation
Courtesy Matthew Marks Gallery

Margi Geerlinks

UNTITLED (GIRL)
1999
Fujichrome, perspex, and dibond
67 x 50 inches

TWINS
2000
Fujichrome, perspex, and dibond
49 1/4 x 60 inches
Courtesy Stefan Stux Gallery

Hilary Harkness

VIEW OF A SLAUGHTER YARD
2000
Oil on panel
13 x 11 3/4 inches
Collection Paul Hertz and James
Rauchman and courtesy Bill
Maynes Gallery

DYING FROM HOME AND LOST
1998
Oil on panel
23 1/2 x 29 inches
Collection David and Leslee
Bogath and courtesy Bill Maynes
Gallery

Claudia Hart

NIGHTMARE FOR TINKY-WINKY
1998
Acrylic on canvas
30 x 60 inches
Courtesy Sandra Gering Gallery

Claudia Hart

A LOVE STORY INVOLVING 2 GUYS
1998
Acrylic on canvas
30 x 60 inches
Courtesy Sandra Gering Gallery

Julie Heffernan

SELF PORTRAIT AS INFANTA DREAM-
ING MADAME DE SADE
1999
Oil on canvas
67 x 58 inches
Collection Janice and Evan Marks
Courtesy Littlejohn Contemporary
and P·P·O·W

Julia Latané

FAIRY RING
1999
Vinyl
192 x 192 x 84 inches

FAIRY RING
1999
Vinyl
120 x 120 x 84 inches
Both courtesy the artist

Tracey Moffatt

INVOCATIONS 13
2000
Photo and silkscreen on paper
48 1/2 x 43 1/2 inches

Tracey Moffatt

INVOCATIONS 9
2000
photo and silkscreen on paper
53 1/2 x 63 inches
Courtesy Matthew Marks Gallery
and Paul Morris Gallery

Maria Porges

WHITE MAGIC
1999
Wood, beeswax, applied text and
image, plexiglass
44 x 34 1/2 x 5 1/2 inches
Courtesy John Berggruen Gallery
and the artist

NAMES OF MAGIC 3
2000
Wood, beeswax, and applied text
21 x 24 x 6 inches
Courtesy David Beitzel Gallery and
the artist

Amy Sillman

FREUDIAN SLIP
2000
Oil on canvas
60 x 50 inches
Collection Gregory Miller
Courtesy Brent Sikkema Gallery

Amy Sillman

TREE
1999
Watercolor and gouache on paper,
mounted on linen
12 x 15 1/2 inches
Courtesy Brent Sikkema Gallery

Elena Sisto

SNOW WHITE
1998
Oil on linen
24 x 36 inches

NOGUE
1998
Oil on linen
26 x 48 inches
Both courtesy Littlejohn Contemporary

I would like to extend my sincere thanks and appreciation to the following lenders, galleries, and individuals whose assistance provided the true magic for *pixerina*WITCHERINA: Karen Arm, Pamela Auchincloss, David Beitzel Gallery, John Berggruen Gallery, David and Leslie Bogath, Bonnie Collura, Amy Cutler, Jody DeCremer, Sandra Gering Gallery, Julie Heffernan, Annie Herron, Paul Hertz, Catherine Hohenzy, Stuart Horodner, Laura Kennedy and WGLT radio, David Kuntz, Julia Latané, Lehmann Maupin Gallery, Littlejohn Contemporary, Bill Maynes Gallery, Bill McBride, Gregory Miller, Paul Morris Gallery, Deborah Purden at Oak Park Bank of Chicago, Janice and Evan Marks, Jeffrey Peabody of Matthew Marks Gallery, Maria Porges, P·P·O·W, James Rauchman, Angie Schmidt and Original Smith Printing, Brent Sikkema Gallery, Amy Sillman, Elena Sisto, Stefan Stux Gallery, Michelle Traver, Roberta Trites, and Eric Yeager.

I cannot thank the University Galleries staff enough for their interest, support, and extensive efforts in realizing this exhibition. Registrar Angela Barker, with her superb shipping, scheduling, and all-round communication skills, contributed much needed enthusiasm to this project. Matt Pulford, Assistant to the Director, provided detailed maintenance for all of the exhibited artworks, assisted in the production of the book, and designed the accompanying web link. Karl Rademacher, Preparator, helped in the installation design and impeccably documented the exhibition. Along with the contribution of a pixie or two, Director Barry Blinderman provided editorial and design assistance. Working under his direction has given me an understanding of the persistence and sensitivity to detail needed to produce such a catalogue. I am especially indebted to Tim Porges, whose masterful editorial input added much color and finesse to my essay.

I also would like to acknowledge Maria Tatar and Jan Susina for their illuminating essays, all the artists in the exhibition for their support, and the Illinois Arts Council, without whose assistance this project could not have been realized.

Loving thanks go to my wife Michelle and our two sons Aiden and Ian, whose literary interests inspired the exhibition. Finally, I am grateful to my grandmother Dorothy Butler, to whose memory this book is dedicated, for providing me with many a magical (and sometimes frightening) saga.

Bill Conger
Curator, University Galleries

ILLINOIS STATE
UNIVERSITY